BREAD RECIPES

Delicious and Easy Recipes for Weight Loss and Healthy Living

(Mouthwatering Gluten Free Bread Recipes to Be Healthy)

Jeremy Cheney

Published by Alex Howard

© **Jeremy Cheney**

All Rights Reserved

Bread Recipes: Delicious and Easy Recipes for Weight Loss and Healthy Living (Mouthwatering Gluten Free Bread Recipes to Be Healthy)

ISBN 978-1-990169-30-4

All rights reserved. No part of this guide may be reproduced in any form without permission in writing from the publisher except in the case of brief quotations embodied in critical articles or reviews.

Legal & Disclaimer

The information contained in this book is not designed to replace or take the place of any form of medicine or professional medical advice. The information in this book has been provided for educational and entertainment purposes only.

The information contained in this book has been compiled from sources deemed reliable, and it is accurate to the best of the Author's knowledge; however, the Author cannot guarantee its accuracy and validity and cannot be held liable for any errors or omissions. Changes are periodically made to this book. You must consult your doctor or get professional medical advice before using any of the suggested remedies, techniques, or information in this book.

Table of contents

PART 1 1

INTRODUCTION 2

CHAPTER 1: GUIDE TO LOW CARB FLOURS AND SWEETENERS FOR BAKING. 4

FLOURS 4
SWEETENERS 6

CHAPTER 2: THE KETO BREAD DEMYSTIFIED 10
PREPARATION 17

CHAPTER 3: KETO BREAD TIPS AND FAQS 19

CHAPTER 4: KETO BREAD RECIPES 32

BREAD 32
KETOGENIC BANANA BREAD 32
SEEDED BREAD LOAF 34
WHITE BREAD WITH COCONUT FLOUR 36
LOW-CARB FOCACCIA BREAD (COCONUT FLOUR) 38
GARLIC CHEESE BREAD LOAF 40
HERBED BREAD LOAF 42

MUFFINS 44
KETO BLUEBERRY MUFFINS 44
KETO CHOCOLATE CHIP MUFFINS 46
KETO COFFEE CAKE MUFFINS 48
KETO PUMPKIN MUFFINS 50
BANANA BREAD MUFFINS 52

CINNAMON MUFFINS	54
CHOCOLATE MUFFINS	56
COFFEE CAKE MUFFINS	58
LEMON POPPYSEED MUFFINS	60

BUNS 62

KETO HAMBURGER BUNS	62
PALEO, KETO BUNS	64
ALMOND BUNS	66
SESAME BUNS	68
LOW-CARB COCONUT HAMBURGER BUNS	70
COOKIES	72
Low-Carb Chocolate Chip Cookies	72
APRICOT AND CREAM CHEESE COOKIES	74
ALMOND BUTTER COOKIES	76
CHOCO HAZELNUT BUTTER COOKIES	78
BANANA WALNUT COOKIES	80

PANCAKES 82

ALMOND BANANA PANCAKES	82
JALAPENO AND CREAM CHEESE PANCAKES	84
COCONUT CHIA PANCAKES	85
KETO BLUEBERRY PANCAKES	87
SPICED PUMPKIN PANCAKES	89
LOW-CARB RED VELVET PANCAKES	90
CITRUS AND RICOTTA PANCAKES	91
KETO BACON AND CHEESE PANCAKES	92

CROISSANTS 94

FRENCH CROISSANT	94

Pumpkin Pie Baked Croissants	96
Quick Croissant	98
Campfire Croissants	100
Almond Croissant Brunch Bake	102
Pizza	104
Cauliflower Pizza Crust	104
Mozzarella Pizza Crust	106
Zucchini Pizza Crust	108
Fat Head Pizza Dough - Egg & Gluten-Free	110
Keto Pizza Pockets	112
Low-Carb Cauliflower Pizza Crust	114
Stovetop Pizza Crust	115
ROLLS	**117**
Low-carb dinner rolls	117
Low-carb clover rolls	119
Keto bread rolls	121
Keto coconut bread rolls	123
Low carb bread rolls (without eggs)	125
CONCLUSION	**127**
PART 2	**128**
INTRODUCTION	**129**
Custard yeast dough for pies	129
Focaccia with filling	130
Ciabatta	131
Bread on kefir, without yeast	131
Lithuanian Homemade bread	133
Wheat-rye bread	134

Carrot and sour cream	135
Bread Armenian festive	136
Indian bread "Puri"	137
Fladenbrot	138
Buckwheat bread	139
Fresh delicious bread bakery	140
Cheese "bread"	141
Steamed bread with balsamic vinegar	142
Mustard Grissini	143
Baursak is round	144
Piglet with cocoa and strawberry jam	145
Borodino bread in the bread maker	146
Wheat-rye yeast bread on brine	147
A fragrant loaf	148
Bread plates	150
Rye bread with oat flakes	151
German festive bread	152
Drunken buns, on beer	153
Wheat corn baguette	154
Just bread	155
Focaccia with cheese from brewed dough	156
"Monkey bread"	157
Pseudo - Borodinsky loaf	158
Long bread	159
Lacy oriental bread	160
Paljanica	161
Cakes with poppy seeds	162
Home Bread "Fitness"	163
Bread Darnytskyi	164

Bread yoghurt-milk with dried fruits 165

Mini-tortillas with eggplant, paprika and olives 166

Basic bread recipe 167

Challah 168

Cat "Matroskin" 169

Dough, pies, pizza 170

Italian bread 171

Italian ciabatta bread 172

Khrushchev's dough sticks 173

Mustard bread 174

Sweet Arabic bread 175

Focaccia with black olives 176

Bread, Mediterranean 177

Christmas bread 178

Tartin with garlic butter 179

ITALIAN BREAD... 181

1. Easy Italian Bread 181

2. Mom's Italian Bread Recipe 183

3. Rustic Italian Bread 184

4. Sourdough Ciabatta Italian Bread 186

5. Italian Cheese Bread **188**

Part 1

Introduction

Bread is a common staple all over the world. Each country has its own special type of bread, so why cut this particular food item out of your diet? Just because you're following the keto diet doesn't mean that you have to stop eating this delicious food. However, you will have to change the types of bread you choose to eat when following this diet.

Keto bread is low in carbs, gluten, and sugar. You can eat lot of it without having to worry about too much sugar or even adding your weight. This is because the flours that make the keto bread lack the regular carbs present in grain flours like wheat.

Since the keto diet consists of foods that are low-carb, high-fat, and moderate in proteins, this means that you have to choose the foods you eat carefully. If you don't want to have to say goodbye to bread forever, you can either choose keto-friendly versions or, better yet, make your own bread. To start off, let's take a look at some of the basic ingredients used in keto baking.

While traditional breads are made with yeast and dairy products, you will find that the substitutions that are used for these keto recipes mimic the chewy and spongy that are found in original recipes. They taste even better and will keep you full.

In this book ill be sharing with you about the varieties of bread that can be enjoyed on keto.

When on a keto lifestyle, you will enjoy the best recipes while you lose weight effortlessly. Who wouldn't want that? I know you want it. This is the reason why you should go for keto bread and enjoy its full benefits. Once you get used to the keto bread, you will never want to eat the other bread because it is sweet and at the same time has several other benefits that come with ketogenic diet.

Chapter 1: Guide to Low Carb Flours and Sweeteners For Baking

Flours

Flour is an important ingredient for baking. However, most types of flour used in non-keto recipes are high in carbohydrates. The good news is that there are some keto-friendly flour alternatives which you can use for your recipes including the following:

Coconut Flour

This type of flour is a by-product of coconut milk. After coconut milk is extracted, coconut meat is left. This is then dried before being finely ground to produce coconut flour - a fine powder which has a similar appearance to wheat flour. Keep in mind that when you use coconut flour, the recipe must also have a lot of eggs or liquids to add moisture to the final product. Coconut flour is an excellent flour substitute if you're allergic to nuts.

Moreover, eggs play a significant role when it comes to baking with coconut flour. Eggs are a binding factor for the ingredients giving a good structure. Failing to use eggs will lead to poor cohesion and ultimately causing your meal to crumble. Use an egg for every quarter cup of coconut flour to get a suitable binding effect.

Coconut flour has a tendency of absorbing liquid quickly. For this reason, you will have to use a little more than the usual recipe. Please do not submerge everything like you trying to replicate some flooded amazon jungle! Lastly you will have to sift the coconut because it can get a bit coarse or clumpy.

Golden Flax Meal

This type of flour is made from finely ground flax seeds. Although it works well in different types of keto baking recipes, it's important to note that it's a heavy type of flour.

Sesame Seed Flour

This is made from finely-ground sesame seeds, and it's another great nut-free alternative. This type of flour isn't very common, but you can make it yourself at home from scratch. Sesame seed flour also has a strong taste so be careful when using this as a replacement in recipes.

Hazelnut Flour

This kind of flour comes from finely ground hazelnuts, and it's an excellent alternative to almond flour. It's less grainy thus producing baked goods with a finer texture. Because of this, hazelnut flour is especially nice in cake and cookie recipes. However, it's one of the more expensive types of low-carb flour options.

Almond Flour and Almond Meal

Almond flour has a light color and texture as it's made from peeled almonds which are finely ground. Before grinding, the almonds are blanched, making it easier to remove the skins. Almond meal looks a lot like almond flour, but the difference is that it has brown-colored flecks in it. This is because almond meal is made from unpeeled almonds. In terms of cost, almond flour is more expensive since it undergoes the blanching process making the production process more labor-intensive.

Sunflower Seed Flour

This is another great alternative for those who are allergic to nuts. Sunflower seed flour is made from ground sunflower seeds. It has a pretty strong taste that varies from one band to another. Therefore, you may have to try out different brands before finding one that you really like.

Sweeteners

Swerve Granular Sweetener

It is also an excellent choice as a blend. It's made from non-digestible carbs sourced from starchy root veggies and select fruits. Start with 3/4 of a tsp for every one of sugar. Increase the portion to your liking. Swerve also has its own confectioners or powdered sugar for your baking needs. On the downside, it is more expensive.

Stevia

Stevia drops include English toffee, hazelnut, vanilla, and chocolate flavors. Stevia is a common herb known as sugar leaf and is available in drops, glycerite, or in powder form. Enjoy making a satisfying cup of sweetened coffee or other favorite drink. Some individuals think the stevia drops are too bitter. At first, use only three drops to equal one tsp of sugar.

Erythritol

This was discovered by chemist John Stenhouse in 1848. The substance occurs naturally in some fruits and mushrooms. It is produced industrially by subjecting starch from corn to enzymatic hydrolysis to yield glucose, which is then fermented using fungus to produce erythritol. This has been used in Japan since the 1990s. It comes in crystal and powdered form, with the latter being more commonly preferred.

It has good taste with minimal aftertaste, and has mild cooling effect on the mouth. It has 0.2 calories per gram, which is 5% the calories of sugar, with 65% sweetness.

Allulose (Psicose)

It is a sugar which has low calorie levels but just as sweet and clean as the expected of sugar.

The existence of allulose is very little in nature because it is available in small volumes. Allulose was found in wheat at first and later on in some particular fruits which included raisins, figs and jackfruit.

For sweet foods such as brown sugar, maple syrup and caramel sauce, allulose occurs in little quantities.

Allulose is a simple sugar (monosaccharide) and the body absorbs it automatically and it is calorie free.

It is ideal for people who want to limit their calorie intake. People do that by taking drinks and foods with low ingredients with low calorie sweeteners like allulose. This is also made possible by the fact that allulose replicates the technical sugar functions in some foods like baked foods and ice cream.

Xylitol

In its refined form, xylitol is a white crystalline substance that resembles table sugar. It comes from the birch tree and is thus classified as a tree sugar, in the same way that maple sugar comes from the maple tree.

What sets this sugar substitute apart is that it has a chemical structure that actually helps the teeth. With table sugar, a fermentation process occurs in the mouth when the saliva dissolves the sugar. Fermentation commonly occurs with wine and other beverages that you want to age. In fermentation, sugar is broken down into an acidic compound because of certain bacteria.

Stevia

Stevia is an aromatic herb originating from South America, especially from Brazil and Paraguay, which has been used since ancient times as a sweetener as well as a medicine in these countries. Stevia is a natural sweetener derived from the leaves of the Stevia rebaudiana plant. It has no calories or carbohydrates and zero glycemic index so it's often used to reduce or replace sugar in recipes. That said, it's about ten to fifteen times sweeter than other natural sweeteners so it doesn't take much stevia to sweeten a recipe. It can also have a slightly bitter aftertaste depending on how it's used and it doesn't caramelize like other sweeteners, so it works best in small amounts and in recipes where there are other sources of sweetness, such as honey, maple syrup, or fruit. The sweetness also varies by brand.

Stevia carries some health benefits, rather than just risks. These include;

1. Positive side effects claimed for Stevia include:
2. Helps balance blood sugar
3. Sweeter than sugar

4. Improves digestion
5. Increases energy levels
6. Can be used to speed healing

Chapter 2: The Keto Bread demystified

Bread ingredients

There are many keto breads for you to bake at home. As a result, there are many varying recipes of keto breads for you to pick from. This probes one question if you give some thought into it. What qualifies a given type of bread as keto bread if so? Although there are many existing recipes of keto breads, there is a given type of consistency in their ingredients. Other ingredients are secondary but a given few are recognized as the building blocks of keto bread.

1. Butter

It is milk fat thus a dairy product. Butter has saturated fats and a higher concentration of calories compared to proteins and carbohydrates. It is very versatile ingredient regardless of the recipe. It can be used in cooking, spreading and baking.

There are also different types of butter used in keto diet. They are clarified butter, grass-fed butter and ghee. Clarified butter is entirely fat without lactose, milk or protein. It is good for an individual who is lactose intolerant. Ghee takes a bit longer to prepare compared to clarified butter. Existing milk solids in it are browned and if kept well, can take a long time before going bad.

Grass-fed butter is the best since it contains higher levels of Conjugated Linoleic Acid compared to commercial butter. This is as a result of the feed given to the cows when owner opts for grass rather than commercial feed. Conjugated Linoleic Acid assists consumers in losing body fat.

When it comes to butter in keto diet, there are specific known brands which are highly recommended. They are Kerrygold, Allgau, Organic Valley and Smjor. You will find them in many keto recipes today for they are grass-fed butter. However, Kerrygold does use commercial feed as substitute for their cow feed in winters. Even so, some of their grass-fed butter would still be available.

2. **Flour**

When baking your keto bread, you can either opt for Almond flour, Almond meal, ground flaxseed, flax meal or coconut flour. Almond flour is obtained from ground almond seeds. In addition to this, Almond flour and Almond meal are two different things. The former involving the removal of the skins while the latter is prepared whole (skins and seeds). It is possible to produce your own almond flour at home. This type of flour is more nutritious than wheat flour being rich in fibers and healthy fats. It is a low-carb and good for baking.

Coconut flour is another alternative to the wheat flour. It is produced from coconut pulp after the raw product has been processed for its milk. Rich in proteins, healthy fats and fiber, coconut flour is good for baking. However, its high fiber concentration makes it denser than regular flour meaning you will have to work with a given ratio. When working on a given recipe requiring you to substitute wheat flour for coconut flour, the ratio will be 1:4. For a cup of regular wheat, you will substitute it with only a quarter cup of coconut flour.

Moreover, eggs play a significant role when it comes to baking with coconut flour. Eggs are a binding factor for the ingredients giving a good structure. Failing to use eggs will lead to poor cohesion and ultimately causing your meal to crumble. Use an egg for every quarter cup of coconut flour to get a suitable binding effect.

Coconut flour has a tendency of absorbing liquid quickly. For this reason you will have to use a little more than the usual recipe. Please do not submerge everything like you trying to replicate some flooded amazon jungle! Lastly you will have to sift the coconut because it can get a bit coarse or clumpy.

Macadamia nuts and flax seeds are other two sources of keto flour. Flaxseeds are rich in dietary fiber and omega 3-fats. When consumed whole (skins and seeds) they are known as flax meal.

3. Sweeteners

Sweeteners can be opted as a substitute for sugar. Contrary though, not all sweeteners are low-carb ones. In fact, there are some sweeteners which contain more carb content than sugar. Honey, a natural sweetener, has more carb content than sugar.

Furthermore, there are sweeteners that can work for some people while others it may result in digestive issues. Xylitol is a good example of such sweeteners. It is a sugar alcohol which may not be a great sugar substitute for every individual in your household. Apart from this, Xylitol can increase blood sugar levels in other persons too.

The sweeteners you can use for baking are stevia, Erythritol and Monk fruit sweetener. They neither bring digestive complications nor increase your blood sugar levels. In addition to this, they are low-carb sweeteners. Although they are versatile and can be used in any recipe, they do have different ratios upon substituting with sugar.

Stevia and Monk fruit sweetener are natural sweeteners as they are obtained from plants. However, some people state that Stevia has a rather bitter aftertaste. On the other hand, Monk fruit sweetener has no aftertaste to it.

Erythritol is a sugar alcohol produced after fermentation of corn or birch. It is 70% to 80% identical to sugar thus you have to compensate more to get the expected sweetness. It has a cooling effect similar to mint but this shouldn't make you worry.

4. Yeast

You will find that the active ingredient in any bread product is going to be the yeast. When properly activated, it will create carbon dioxide that is required for the bread to grow in size. This is due to the air pockets that are created by the carbon dioxide which are held in by the stretchy properties of the dough itself.

You cannot see it, but the carbon dioxide reproduces multiple thousands of times in each bread product. It is why the bread will grow noticeably larger in size when left to properly rise before and during baking.

Before the baking process, you will see the largest difference in the expansion of the bread. This process continues when heat is applied after the initial rising process. While the bread is baking, it permanently traps the carbon dioxide that was trapped in the dough and grows a little larger and will keep its shape after being removed from the heat.

You will find that the bread loaves will have larger air pockets in comparison to muffins. This is due to the different textures of the bread products. This is why it is harder to get bread loaves to rise versus smaller items such as biscuits and muffins.

Dry Active Yeast

This is used in a couple of the recipes and requires the most patience. These recipes may pop out to you as they include the ingredient of honey. Before you think that I have made a mistake, honey is purposefully mixed with the yeast so that it can properly activate. The yeast requires the sugars that are present in the honey to create the needed carbon dioxide to perform the rising capabilities.

Through the baking process, this sugar is burned off, much like the process involved with cooking with alcohol. You know that the yeast is doing its job when it starts to froth in the bowl after the 7 minutes has passed for it to activate.

If you have problems with the yeast bubbling, it is due to the water not being the correct temperature. If you have the water hotter than 110° Fahrenheit, then you have actually killed the yeast preventing it from activating. If the water is cooler than 105°, then it is not hot enough to activate the yeast in the first place. Both of the results mean you need to start the process of warming the water yet again. Avoid having to repeat the steps by having a kitchen thermometer handy to ensure this finicky component will work properly. You will find that this process takes much longer than the other more common ingredient used in leavening bread.

5. Baking Soda

You may remember science class where you had the replica of the volcano where you had baking soda and red food coloring inside and poured simple vinegar inside the well. Immediately the volcano erupted with all the red lava glory.

This is what is happening with your bread on a smaller and much less messy scale. As you can see from this illustration, the baking soda used in the Keto diet breads have a much quicker rising process and does not need to be monitored as in the case of the dry active yeast. This is why this is the preferred way of modern bread making.

Bread machines

As you can see, there are so many ingredients you can use for your baking (and cooking) while on this diet. As long as you have these basic ingredients in your kitchen, you can stick with it long-term. Apart from the basic ingredients, there are also a number of basic tools you would need for keto baking. Some of these basic tools include the following:

- Baking sheets
- Cake pans
- Cookie scoops
- Cooling racks
- Food processor

- Hand mixer
- Loaf pans
- Measuring bowls (made of stainless steel)
- Measuring cups
- Measuring spoons
- Parchment paper
- Rolling pins
- Silicone baking mats
- Spatulas
- Stand-up mixer
- Whisks

Start off with a few basic tools and you can begin building your baking arsenal over time so you can create more complex recipes which require additional ingredients.

Homemade bread

When you're starting on the keto diet and you plan to bake your own bread, it's helpful for you to know the most basic keto bread recipe. The great thing about keto baking is that there are so many food items you can create using simple ingredients - and a lot of the recipes (as you will see later on) have similar ingredients. This means that if you really plan to do a lot of baking, there are certain ingredients that you may want to consider buying in bulk as you will be using them for different recipes.

When it comes to keto baking, it is ideal for you to start off with the simplest, easiest recipes so you can get the hang of the whole process. This allows you to familiarize yourself with the basic keto-friendly ingredients before you start creating more elaborate dishes.

Properties of bread

The major property of the keto bread is that it is low in carbs. This is what makes it keto.

Bread can be eaten during breakfast or any time of the day as a snack or a dessert. It is popular because it can be made and eaten several times.

Preparation

If you don't have baking powder, you can invent your own by including baking soda and lemon juice or citric acid. The ratio of baking soda to citric acid is 2:1. For lemon juice you will go with 2 tbsps for a single tsp of baking soda. However, don't change the quantities if the recipe has already provided it for you. Always make sure to directly add lemon juice on the baking soda for it to react well. You may opt to do this on the side before mixing all the ingredients.

When you're starting on the keto diet and you plan to bake your own bread, it's helpful for you to know the most basic keto bread recipe. The great thing about keto baking is that there are so many food items you can create using simple ingredients - and a lot of the recipes (as you will see later on) have similar ingredients. This means that if you really plan to do a lot of baking, there are certain ingredients that you may want to consider buying in bulk as you will be using them for different recipes.

When it comes to keto baking, it is ideal for you to start off with the simplest, easiest recipes so you can get the hang of the whole process. This allows you to familiarize yourself with the basic keto-friendly ingredients before you start creating more elaborate dishes.

Leavening of bread

Leaving is the process where gas is added to the dough when baking to make the bread or what is being baked or prepared to rise. Leavening of bread is very important in baking.

There are different leavening agents which produce air that makes the bread to rise. These different agents produce air in different ways.

There are thee major kinds of leavening agent. They are steam, chemical and biological.

Chapter 3: Keto bread tips and FAQs

Keto Bread Tips

Baking Tips

Do not get frustrated if a dish does not turn out perfectly as you are baking with new ingredients which are usually fussy and will take some practice. However, read through these tips carefully to gain the knowledge that you will require to have your Keto breads turn out to be a success!

Temperature is everything

You want to use eggs, cream cheese, sour cream, milk and any other cooled items set at room temperature. This is due to cold items not mixing particularly well into the almond and coconut flours which are used in Keto and if they are not brought down to room temperature, then your bread will not properly rise.

A trick for the eggs, in particular, is to use a bowl of warm water to immerse the eggs for the duration of 4 minutes. This will quickly bring them to room temperature which is a nice trick in case you forgot to pull them out of the fridge.

Make sure that you measure your ingredients properly

This will lead to consistent results for all the Keto recipes that you find. The correct method in measuring is to spoon the ingredient into the cup rather than scooping it out of the bag directly. This will create perfect results every time as you will not over pack the ingredients using this method. You can also ensure that all the ingredients are the correct increments if you purchase a simple kitchen or baking scale.

Ensure the yeast is properly proofed

Not every recipe includes dry active yeast. However, for the ones that do, there is a specific process to follow as outlined in those particular recipes. It includes combining the yeast with honey for the yeast to feed upon. Do not worry about the sugar content as the honey is for the yeast to feed upon, creating the carbon dioxide required for the bread to rise. The sugar will be cooked off during the process and will not be present in the final result.

Once combined, you will blend water which is the specific temperature of 105° - 110° which can be checked with a kitchen thermometer or it will be slightly warm to the touch. You will know that this process was successful by the mixture becoming bubbly after waiting for a period of 7 minutes.

If there are no bubbles, simply repeat the process with the correct temperature water. You will not waste a whole dish because this occurs at the beginning of the recipe.

Temperature is important during the rising process

You want to keep your rising bread in an environment where the temperature is not going to vary much and will be undisturbed during the rising time. You want to have the area to be slightly warm and humid, but not hot as this will stop the rising process. It is suggested to keep the covered tray on top of the stove which is preheating.

Always Sift Your Coconut Flour:

Not sifting your coconut flour will result in a grainy bread full of coconut flour clumps…yuck! To sift your coconut flour, simply use a mesh strainer, and add the coconut flour. Sift over a large container or bowl.

Keep away from xylitol

When using any yeast in your recipes, you want to make sure that xylitol is not an additive in your ingredients as it rapidly decreases the rising of the dough and will cause them to become flat. You will find that Monk Fruit and Erythritol do not contain xylitol and may be used as a substitute for sweeteners that have this additive included.

Loaf pan size is important

There are a wide variety of baking pans out there. I have made it easy by including the particular pan that is required for each recipe. However, if you do not have that specific size, always opt to go with a pan that is the next size up rather than downsizing. This will ensure that the dough will not rise too far causing the bread to burst over the pan.

The measurements for pans are calculated from the top of the pan and does not include the pan itself.

Pure ingredients are everything

Especially when dealing with the different varieties of cheese, you want to make sure there are no preservatives or additives. Also, opt for the skim or whole milk types as these will have less water to weep during the baking process.

When baking powder is being used, it is a priority to ensure that it is as fresh as possible. Since there is no gluten present, it needs to be of the best quality to make the rising process work properly.

Not sure if your baking powder is still active? Do a small test by combining with boiling water. If bubbles occur immediately, then your baking powder will make your bread properly rise.

A perfect way to grease any pan

If you want to make sure that you do not run into the problem of your Keto breads sticking to the pan, this fail-proof trick will take the headache out of baking. Dissolve 2 tsps. of coconut oil in a saucepan and then apply to your pan with a pastry brush. Set in the freezer for a minimum of 20 minutes as the oil hardens. Pull out of the freezer before filling with your dough.

Separating the eggs is a necessary step

It may seem like a pain at the time, but there is a reason that you will find the eggs are separated. This simple measure also helps the Keto breads to rise. When incorporating the whipped eggs into the batter, do not over mix. This is due to you counteracting the airiness that has been created by whipping the eggs and your breads will not rise properly.

For the bread loaves

If you find that your bread is crumbling when you are slicing, ensure the loaf is completely cooled. This will help the bread to set and firm up more when given the time to come to room temperature.

For the muffins

If you are having trouble with your muffins rising properly, add a combination of baking soda and vinegar which causes the carbon dioxide reaction required for proper rising. You will also find that many of the recipes already incorporate this trick.

Tips for the cookies

Different people enjoy cookies hard or soft. Luckily there is a trick in Keto baking which lets you have a choice. The biggest trick is to have the treats completely cool so that the cookie will not crumble.

If you like to have softer cookies, leave them on the countertop in a lidded container or cookie jar. They will keep fresh for up to 5 days. Refrigerate the cookies after they are completely cooled in a covered tub and they will become harder. They will keep for up to 7 days this way.

If your cookies are not rising the way you prefer, simply combine a half tsp of apple cider vinegar while blending the batter. You will find some of the recipes already utilize this trick.

For the Bagels:

Coconut creates bagels that are denser. On the other hand, almond flour creates a light bagel. You can substitute whichever flour for the result that you prefer.

Tips for Saving Time

The keto diet doesn't have to be either complicated or difficult. Although more and more keto-friendly products and food items are being made available these days, it's always better to cook your meals and bake goods at home. Though it might seem odd at the beginning, once you get the hang of things, this process will become faster, easier, and more enjoyable. Since this book is all about baking, here are some time-saving tips for you:

Make riced cauliflower in bulk then use airtight containers to freeze it. That way, you can simply take the amount you need when your recipe calls for it.

For recipes that call for boiled low-carb food items, use an instant pot. This allows you to cook ingredients in bulk faster.

Stock up on parchment paper as you can use this to line your baking sheets, pans, and other similar items before placing them in the oven.

Use your freshly-baked bread loaves to make scrumptious sweet or savory sandwiches. Then store these in the refrigerator for meals on-the-go.

When planning which recipes to bake, check the ingredients to see if they share common items. This makes shopping a lot easier, especially if you want to make meal prepping part of your keto journey.

Tips for Saving Money

Apart from saving time, there are also things you can do in order to save money while following the keto diet. Starting a new diet is always challenging, no matter what type of diet you choose to follow. Most of the time, you won't even know where to start. Although you've already learned all that you can about the diet, actually taking the first step towards starting it can be very intimidating.

If you want to stick with your keto journey, then you must make sure that you don't break the bank just because of it. Otherwise, you might end up deciding that the diet isn't working for you since you're losing money on it. This doesn't have to be the case!

To help you out, here are some clever money-saving tips you can try:

Create things from scratch

Whether you're baking pastries or cooking dishes, it's important to learn how to create things from scratch. Although it's easier and more convenient to purchase ready-made, prepackaged keto food products, doing so will surely make you lose a lot of money. If you want to stick with your budget, learning how to make homemade meals from scratch is of the essence.

Purchase fresh, whole ingredients

Buying ingredients which are fresh and whole allows you to whip up healthy meals and snacks that fit right into your keto diet. In fact, a proper keto diet should be built around these types of ingredients so you can get high-quality sources of macros and the rest of the nutrients. Also, fresh and whole ingredients are a lot cheaper which means that you can save a lot of money.

Buy local produce, which is in season

Do research on which foods and food items are available each season. Purchasing local produce that is in season allows you to get the ingredients you need at an affordable price. As long as you know which ingredients are in season in your locale, you can start planning your meals and recipes easily and more effectively.

Buy ingredients in bulk

Speaking of saving money on ingredients, buying in bulk also allows you to save some money. Go around your locale and check out all the food shops, supermarkets, farmer's markets, and convenience stores. That way, you can determine which places offer the freshest ingredients, which ones have the best prices, and which places offer bulk or wholesale products.

Bake (and cook) in bulk

Of course, if you buy in bulk, it's a good idea to use these ingredients in bulk too. This is where meal prepping comes in. Once a week, set aside some time to plan your meals, shop for all of the ingredients and bake/cook all of your meals for the whole week. This is an excellent way to save money and ensure that you don't feel tempted to buy takeout or ready-made foods, which are less healthy and more expensive.

The bottom line is this: when you start the keto diet, keep in mind that this involves a lot of planning. All of these tips can help make your journey easier so you don't have to feel like you're being constantly challenged. When you see how much time and money you're saving, this can even become your motivation to stick with the diet long-term.

Maintaining a Low-Carb Diet

Although starting the low-carb keto diet may help you lose weight, there are some things for you to consider. First of all, if you really want to shed those unwanted pounds and enjoy all of the health benefits the keto diet has to offer, you must follow it properly. As stated previously, this diet does come with restrictions and you should make sure that you follow them religiously.

Also, to stay on the safe side, you may want to consult with your doctor before you start this diet. This is especially true for people who are suffering from medical conditions or for those who have a complicated medical history. If you've already made the decision to go low-carb, here are some pointers for you:

Choose your carbs wisely

The main energy sources of the body come from simple and complex carbs. Simple carbs are those naturally found in milk and fruits, but sweets such as candies also contain them. When choosing foods which contain carbs, opt for the complex variety such as starchy veggies, lentils, beans, and legumes.

Opt for lean protein

Just because you're allowed to eat moderate amounts of protein while on the keto diet, this doesn't mean that you should eat all kinds of protein. If you want to lose weight and improve your health, then the best protein choices are eggs, beans, skinless turkey or chicken breast, and fish.

Make it a habit to read food labels

This allows you to choose the ingredients and food items which fit into your diet more effectively. When you read food labels, this gives you information about the food items you plan to purchase from stores.

Consume a lot of non-starchy veggies and fruits

Although these food items may contain simple carbs, that doesn't mean you should stop eating them. Fruits and veggies are the healthiest kinds of foods, so continue eating them as part of your diet to ensure your overall health.

Plan your meals

Meal planning can be your friend when you're following the keto diet. This involves planning your meals for a specific amount of time (like for one week), shopping for ingredients, then setting one day each week to cook all of the meals you've planned. It's an excellent way to save time, money, and to stick with your diet.

Maintain open communication with your doctor

Finally, it's important to maintain open communication with your doctor, especially when you experience any changes because of the diet. Whether you're at the peak of your health or you're suffering from any kind of medical condition, keeping your doctor in the loop is essential.

Learn How to Check Nutritional Information

As mentioned, it's important to check food labels. In fact, you should make this a habit if you decide to start the keto diet. The good news is that all of the big food companies have introduced new nutrition labels which makes it easier to learn the nutritional information of the foods you plan to buy. Here are some steps to follow when checking nutritional information:

Check the serving size

This information tells you how many calories and nutrients you would get for each serving of the food item. When you know this, you can compare this serving size with the amount you actually consume.

Check the caloric information

This information tells you the amount of energy you obtain for each serving.

Check the percent daily value

This information tells you the percentage of nutrients on a scale which, in turn, tells you if the food item contains minimal or high amounts of nutrients. A DV of 5% and below is considered little and a DV of 15% and above is considered a lot.

Search for these nutrients

Look for calcium, fiber, iron, vitamin A, and vitamin C.

Conversely, try to avoid these

Cholesterol, fat, saturated fat, sodium, and trans fat.

The great thing about nutrition labels is these make it easier to compare products, they allow you to find out the nutritional value of food items, and they help you determine whether or not different food items are appropriate for your diet.

FAQs

What is the difference between a ketogenic diet and a low-carb diet?

Low carb diet is a general term used to describe any diet containing 130 to 150 grams on the total. However ketogenic diets are the subset of this general diet plan. It further restricts the amount of carbohydrate to minimum levels and at the same time requires an increased intake of fat. Thus, a ketogenic diet plan is more specific than the low carbohydrate plan.

Do I need to count calories? Are calories of importance?

Keeping track of caloric intake is important as it directly relates to weight gain. Whether on a low carb diet or on a high one, it is necessary to keep check of the calories.

How can a person track carb intake/ macro?

Whenever you follow a recipe, look for its contents and the nutritional value available with the recipe. If it is not available, look for online nutrition calculators which enables you to calculate the nutritional value within few minutes.

What is the time taken to get to ketosis?

If you are a person of discipline and routine then it typically takes two to three days to start a keto routine. However, it is a gradual process and goes through different stages. Exercise helps boosts the speed of the process. For people with sedentary lifestyles, it can also take weeks.

Can I eat dairy?

This is perhaps the most frequently asked question by the people who are new to a keto diet. Not all dairy products are keto friendly as raw dairy products are high in carbs. But those fermented or processed loses their carbohydrates and are good to use, these include butter, cheese and yoghurt.

Can I eat peanuts?

Not all legumes are not keto friendly, peanuts are one of them. There is a great misconception that peanuts can be taken on a keto diet, but it is clearly not true as they are low on carbs and high in fats. When taken in small amounts, they do not disrupt the balance of the ketogenic diet.

Is ketosis bad?

There is no proven evidence which could suggest that ketosis is dangerous. Many people confuse ketosis with the ketoacidosis, the latter is a health problem which only occurs in patients with diabetes type 1. During ketoacidosis, the ketones level in the blood exceeds up to a critical value. Ketosis, on the other hand, is completely normal and doesn't pose any danger to a person's health.

Are the high-fat foods healthy? Does eating a lot of fat make people fat?

Most of us believe that high fats are unhealthy but it is nothing but a myth. Fats can only be unhealthy if taken with the high amount of carbohydrates. However, when taken with low carbs or no carbs, these fats become a direct and active source of energy for the body. They easily break down and releases essential compounds including ketones.

Can I go off of the ketogenic diet plan and still keep the weight off?

Unfortunately, when you see-saw on any diet plan, you're going to gain the weight back. Some individuals don't understand that you're making a lifestyle change.

Do I have to fast while on the ketogenic diet plan?

It's not a requirement. If you ease into the process of fasting as described in this book, you can lower your carbohydrates slowly. Although, if you add the intermittent fasting plan as described, you can also accelerate your weight loss, help hunger control, and cravings as well as detoxification.

Chapter 4: Keto Bread Recipes

Bread

Ketogenic Banana Bread

Prep minutes 10 / Cook 40 minutes / Serves 4/ 355ºF/ Serves: 4

Difficulty: Beginner

PER SEVING: Calories: 164; Fat: 14g; Saturated Fat: 4g; Protein: 6g; Carbohydrates: 4g; Sodium: 121mg; Fiber: 1g; Sugar: 1g

Ingredients

5 eggs

2 tbsps. carbquik

3 tsps. baking powder

1 cup chopped pecans

1 tbsp vanilla sugar-free syrup

¾ cup granular Splenda

3 tsps. banana extract

Directions

Put all ingredients in a blender mixing on HIGH once every addition.

Ensure that the pecans are finely blended as they will be the "flour".

Add the batter in an 8x4" loaf pan which is lubricated. Bake for 40 minutes at 355ºF-.

Cool on a rack before serving.

Seeded Bread Loaf

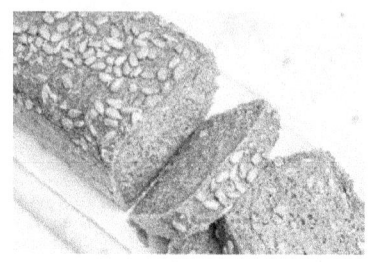

Prep 10 minutes / Cook 50 minutes / Serves 20/ 340ºF

Difficulty: Intermediate

PER SEVING: Calories: 161; Fat: 12.7g; Saturated Fat: 2.1g; Protein: 6.5g; Carbohydrates: 3.6g; Sodium: 56mg; Fiber: 3g; Sugar: 2g;

Ingredients

1 ½ cup almond flour

1 cup sunflower seeds

½ cup chia seeds

½ tsp salt

1 cup pumpkin seeds

2 tbsps. olive oil

1 cup sesame seeds

5 eggs, preferably farm-raised

Directions

Preheat the oven to 340ºF.

Place the almond flour and the eggs in a food processor and blend once.

To this, add the seeds, olive oil, and salt and pulse the mixture again until the seeds are broken down into small bits. Don't blend the dough for too long, as the bread won't be crunchy.

Next, line the loaf pan with parchment paper and transfer the dough into it. Shape as needed.

Now, bake the bread 48 to 50 minutes or until the top portion is lightly browned.

Allow the bread to cool completely before slicing. Tip: slice it thinly as the bread is dense.

You can serve the bread either by toasting it with butter or as a base for fried eggs.

White Bread with Coconut Flour

Prep 12 minutes/ Cook 12 minutes / Serves 4/ 350ºF

Difficulty: Intermediate

PER SEVING: Calories: 307; Fat: 11g; Saturated Fat: 2.1g; Protein: 4g; Carbohydrates: 4g; Sodium: 408mg; Fiber: 0.7g; Sugar: 0g

Ingredients

½ cup coconut flour

1 tsp baking powder

¼ tsp salt

6 eggs (lightly beaten)

½ cup butter(melted)

Directions

Preheat oven to 350ºF. spray Associate in Nursing 8" x 4" loaf pan with slippery change of state spray and put aside.

In a small bowl, mix coconut flour, baking powder, and salt until thoroughly combined and set aside.

In a large bowl, beat eggs with an electric hand mixer until frothy. Continue beating and slowly add butter to eggs in a thin stream and beat until thoroughly combined. Continue beating and add dry ingredients to egg mixture and beat until thoroughly combined.

Pour batter into ready 8 x 4" pan and bake for 45 minutes. Let bread cool in pan on a wire rack for 10 minutes. Remove bread from pan to cool completely and slice to serve. Enjoy!

Low-carb Focaccia Bread (coconut flour)

Prep 15 minutes / Cook 30 12 minutes / Serves 1/ 356ºF

Difficulty: Expert

PER SERVING: Calories 348, Total Fat 9.5g, Saturated Fat 4.4g, Sodium 768mg, Total Carbohydrate 70.6g, Dietary Fiber 51.3g, Sugars 0.4g, Protein 12.3g,

Ingredients

5.3-ounce (50g) coconut flour

5 eggs

2 tsps. baking powder

1 tsp salt

5 tbsps. psyllium husk

250ml hot water

Directions

Using a mixing bowl first put your coconut flour. Add psyllium husk, baking powder, salt and mix the contents in the bowl.

Add eggs into the bowl and mix. The content at this point will be less workable but don't worry about it.

Add the hot water and work on the mixture thoroughly.

Align your baking tray with baking paper. Make a focaccia shape out of the dough, put it on the baking tray and make lateral cuts on the dough.

Add olives on top. Sprinkle some rosemary and salt in the cuts.

For 30min, bake it at 356ºF. The center of the bread shouldn't be spongy when you remove it. That's how you know it's ready. You can serve it with butter then or use tomatoes, cheese, avocadoes etc. when it's cool.

Garlic Cheese Bread Loaf

Prep 12 minutes/ Cook 50 minutes / Serves 10/ 355ºF

Difficulty: Intermediate

PER SERVING: Calories: 299; Fat: 3g; Saturated Fat: 1g; Protein: 11g; Carbohydrates: 4g; Sodium: 121mg; Fiber: 1g; Sugar: 0g

Ingredients

1 tbsp. parsley seasoning

0.5 cup butter, unsalted and softened

2 tbsp garlic powder

6 large eggs

0.5 tbsp oregano seasoning

1 tsp baking powder, gluten-free

2 cup almond flour

0.5 tsp xanthan gum

1 cup cheddar cheese, shredded

0.5 tsp salt

Directions

Set your stove to heat at the temperature of 355ºF.

Utilize baking lining to cover a 9 x 5-inch bread loaf pan

pan and set to the side.

Use a food blender to pulse the eggs until smooth. Combine the butter and pulse for an additional 60 seconds until integrated.

Blend the almond flour and baking powder for approximately 90 more seconds until the batter thickens.

Finally combine the oregano, garlic, parsley, and cheese until integrated.

Distribute into the prepped pan and smooth evenly with a scraper.

For approximately 45 minutes, heat the bread and check with a utensil to ensure it has baked properly when it comes out without residue.

Transfer to the countertop and wait about 15 minutes before slicing and serving.

Herbed Bread Loaf

Prep 10 minutes /Cook 60 minutes /Serves 12/ 350ºF

Difficulty: Expert

PER SERVING: Calories: 127; Fat: 10g; Saturated Fat: 1g; Protein: 6g; Carbohydrates: 0.5g; Sodium: 116mg; Fiber: 3g; Sugar: 1g

Ingredients

2.5 cups almond flour

8 oz. cream cheese, full-fat

1.5 tsp baking powder, gluten-free

0.25 cup coconut flour

0.5 cup butter, unsalted

1 tsp rosemary seasoning

8 whole eggs

1 tsp sage seasoning

2 tbsp parsley seasoning

3 tsp butter, unsalted and separate

Directions

Heat the stove at a temperature of 350ºF.

Prepare a 8 x 4-inch bread loaf pan thoroughly with one tbsp. of butter and set to the side.

Blend the cream cheese and the leftover ½ cup of butter in a food blender for approximately 45 seconds until the consistency is smooth.

Combine the parsley, sage, and rosemary into the blender and pulse for another half minute until integrated.

Whip one egg in the blender until combined. Repeat for the other 7 eggs until complete.

Finally, blend the coconut flour, baking powder, and almond flour for an additional 90 seconds until the batter is a thick consistency.

Distribute to the prepped pan evenly while smoothing with a scraper.

Utilize a utensil to see if any residue remains after poking into the center.

Transfer to the countertop and wait approximately 15 minutes before dividing and serving.

Muffins

Keto blueberry muffins

Prep 10 minutes/ Cook 25 minutes / Serves 12/ 360ºF

Difficulty: Beginner

PER SERVING: Calories: 124; Carbohydrates: 5g; Fat: 7g; saturated fat: 2g; Sodium: 154mg; Fiber: 2g; Protein: 3g

Ingredients

1/3 cups keto friendly sugar

1 ½ tsps. baking powder

½ tsp baking soda

½ cups almond flour

½ tsp kosher salt

1/3 cups butter, melted

1/3 cups almond milk

3 Large eggs

1 tsp pure vanilla extract

2/3 cups fresh blueberries

Directions

Preheat the oven to 360ºF.

Line your Pan size: 15.75"x 11.25" muffin pan with cupcake liners or grease it.

Add almond flour, sugar, baking powder, baking soda, and salt to a bowl then whisk to combine

Add your wet ingredients, that is, the melted butter, almond milk, eggs and vanilla extract to another bowl then mix.

Add butter mixture to the mixture of dry ingredients then stir to mix.

Gently fold in your blueberries.

Scoop batter onto the muffin pan to a level of about ¾.

Bake for about 25 minutes.

Insert a toothpick into a muffin. If the muffins are ready, it should come out clean.

Allow to cool for 5-10 minutes.

Keto chocolate chip muffins

Prep 10/ Cook 20/ Serves 6/ 350ºF

Difficulty: Intermediate

PER SERVING: Calories: 229; Fat: 12g; Saturated Fat: 2g; Protein: 7g; Carbohydrates: 11g; Sodium: 96mg; Fiber: 0g; Sugar: 2g

Ingredients

1 Cup Almond Flour

2 large eggs

1 tsp baking powder

¼ cup Erythritol

40g Butter (melted)

40 ml unsweetened almond milk

1 tsp Vanilla Extract

50g (Unsweetened) Dark Chocolate

Directions

Preheat your oven to a temperature of 350ºF.

Line your 13.75"x 10.5" muffin pan with cupcake liners or grease it.

Mix the almond flour and the baking powder together in a bowl.

Add 2 eggs into the bowl and stir to mix.

Melt the butter then add into the bowl.

Add the other ingredients (apart from the chocolate) and whisk.

Spoon the batter into your muffin tray filling it up to a level of ¾.

Cut the pieces of chocolate into thin slices.

Pierce them through the top of the muffins.

Bake for 20 minutes. A toothpick should come out clean when poked through the muffin.

Let them cool for 5-10 minutes.

Keto coffee cake muffins

Prep 20 minutes/ Cook 25 minutes/ Serves 12/ 3555ºF

Difficulty: Intermediate

PER SERVING: Calories: 222; Total Fat: 18g; Cholesterol: 72mg; Sodium:156mg; Protein: 7g; Potassium: 73mg; Carbohydrates: 9g

Ingredients

2 tbsps. butter softened

2 ounces cream cheese softened

1 tsp baking powder

¼ cup tsp salt

1/3 cup Swerve

2 tsp vanilla

½ cup unsweetened almond milk

1 cup almond flour

½ cup coconut flour

4 eggs

(Topping)

1 tsp cinnamon

2 tbsps coconut flour

¼ cup Swerve

¼ cup butter softened

1 cup almond flour

Ingredients

Preheat oven to 355ºF. Line a muffin tin with paper liners or grease the muffin tin.

Place cream cheese, vanilla and eggs in a food processor and blend until well combined.

Put the dry ingredients to a big bowl and thoroughly mix.

Combine the dry and wet ingredients and whisk.

For the topping add your ingredients together in a separate bowl and mix.

Bake 25 minutes until golden. When you insert toothpick, it should come out clean.

Keto pumpkin muffins

Prep 10 minutes/ Cook 20 minutes/ Serves 16/ 350ºF

Difficulty: Beginner

PER SERVING: Calories: 121; Carbohydrates:3g; Protein: 2g; Fat: 10g; Cholesterol: 55mg; Sodium: 116mg; Potassium: 95mg; Fiber: 1g

Ingredients

5 eggs

½ cup liquid coconut oil

2 tbsp butter

1 cup pumpkin puree

1 ½ tbsp. pumpkin pie spice

1 ½ cup Swerve

2 tsps. vanilla extract

½ cup coconut flour

1 tsp salt

1 ½ tsps. baking powder

Filling

2 ounces cream cheese

2 tbsps heavy whipping cream

1 tbsps swerve or sweetener of your choice

1 tsp vanilla extract

Directions

Preheat oven to 350ºF then grease the 15.75" x 11.25"muffin pan or line it with muffin liners.

Melt the butter.

Add eggs, coconut oil, melted butter, pumpkin puree, pumpkin pie spice, swerve and vanilla extract to a large bowl and mix until well combined.

Add coconut flour, salt and baking powder to the other ingredients and mix.

Scoop batter into prepared muffin tins, filling each one 3/4 way.

In another bowl, add the ingredients for the filling and stir until well combined and smooth.

Place 1 tsp of filling in the center of each muffin.

Using a toothpick swirl cream cheese batter into muffin

Bake for 20 minutes.

Notes: these muffins need a thicker batter than most muffins do.

Banana Bread Muffins

Prep 10 minutes/ Cook 25 minutes/ Serves 6/ 350ºF

Difficulty: Beginner

PER SERVING: Calories: 184; Carbohydrates:4g; Protein: 7g; Fat: 14g; Cholesterol: 23mg; Sodium: 43mg; Potassium: 95mg; Fiber: 1g; Sugar: 1g

Ingredients

0.125 cup Erythritol sweetener, confectioner

0.75 cup almond flour

1.25 tbsp ground flax

3 tbsp butter, unsalted and melted

0.125 cup sour cream, full-fat

1.25 tsp baking powder, gluten-free

4 oz. walnuts, raw and chopped

0.33 tsp ground cinnamon

2 tsp butter, unsalted, cubed and separate

1.5 tsp banana extract, sugar-free

2 tsp almond flour, separate

0.125 cup almond milk, unsweetened

1 tsp vanilla extract, sugar-free

2 tsp Erythritol sweetener, confectioner and separate

1 large egg

Directions

Dissolve the 3 tsp. of butter completely in a 6.5" saucepan and set to the side.

Adjust the temperature of the stove to heat at 350ºF. Line a small cupcake tin with 6 papers or silicone cups. Set aside.

Use a food blender to pulse the 2 tsp. of almond flour, 2 tsp. of butter and walnuts until a crumbly consistency. Set to the side.

Blend the 1/3 cup of Erythritol, cinnamon, baking powder and ¾ cup of almond flour until incorporated fully.

Combine the eggs, sour cream, banana extract, almond milk, melted butter, and vanilla extract into the mixture until integrated.

Evenly distribute to the prepped cupcake tin and dust with the crumble from the food processor. Apply slight pressure to adhere to the batter.

Evenly spread the 2 tsp. of Erythritol over the muffins.

Heat for a total of 20 minutes and take out of the stove to the countertop.

Wait about half an hour before serving. Enjoy!

Cinnamon Muffins

Prep 11 minutes / Cook 20 minutes / Serves 12/ 350ºF

Difficulty: Beginner

PER SERVING: Calories: 89; Fat: 9g; Saturated Fat: 2g; Protein: 5g; Carbohydrates: 1.8g; Sodium: 132mg; Fiber: 0g; Sugar: 2g

Ingredients

For the muffin:

0.33 cup almond flour

0.5 tsp baking powder, gluten-free

0.33 cup almond butter

0.5 tbsp ground cinnamon

5 oz. pumpkin puree

0.33 cup coconut oil

12 cavity muffin tin or 24 cavity mini muffin tin

For the optional topping:

0.125 cup coconut butter

0.5 tbsp. Swerve sweetener, granulated

0.125 cup milk

1.25 tsp. lemon juice

Directions

Set your stove to heat at the temperature of 350ºF.

Use silicone or baking cups to line your preferred cupcake tin. Set to the side.

Combine the almond flour, baking powder, and cinnamon with a whisk in a glass dish. Remove any lumpiness present.

Blend the almond butter, pumpkin puree, and coconut oil into the mix until incorporated.

Evenly divide the batter between the cavities in the prepped cupcake tin.

Heat for approximately 13 minutes and transfer to a wire rack after waiting 5 minutes.

If you are applying the topping, blend the lemon juice, milk, Swerve, and coconut butter until smooth.

Evenly empty the topping once the muffins have completely cooled.

Chocolate Muffins

Prep 15 minutes / Cook 30 minutes / Serves 12/ 350ºF

Difficulty: Beginner

PER SERVING: Calories: 189; Protein: 7g; Net carbohydrates: 3.5g; Fat: 16g; Sugar: 1g

Ingredients

0.5 tsp salt

2 cups almond flour, blanched

0.5 cup cocoa powder, unsweetened

0.75 cup Pyure Stevia blend, granulated

1 tsp. baking powder, gluten-free

4 large eggs

0.25 cup coconut oil, melted

2 oz. almond milk, unsweetened

1 tsp vanilla extract, sugar-free

1.75 oz. dark chocolate, Stevia sweetened and chopped

Directions

Set the temperature of the stove to heat at 350ºF. Cover the cavities of the cupcake tin with baking liner or silicone. Set to the side.

Liquefy the coconut oil for approximately 3 minutes in a saucepan.

Chop the chocolate roughly into small chunks and set aside.

Blend the salt, baking powder, almond flour, Pyure Stevia blend, and cocoa powder until fully incorporated.

Combine the melted coconut oil, vanilla extract, almond milk, and eggs into the mix and toss until integrated.

Finally, incorporate the chopped chocolate into the mix.

Evenly divide the batter to the prepped cupcake tin.

For the duration of approximately 26 minutes, heat the muffins and then transfer to the countertop.

Wait about 10 minutes before serving and enjoy!

Coffee Cake Muffins

Prep 10 minutes/ Cook 30 minutes/ Serves 12/ 325ºF

Difficulty: Intermediate

PER SERVING: Calories: 284; Protein: 9g; Net carbohydrates: 3.9g; Fat: 24g; Sugar: 1g

Ingredients

For the muffins:

0.5 tsp ground cinnamon

2 cups almond flour

0.5 cup almond milk, unsweetened

0.33 cup Swerve sweetener, granulated

3 tbsp coconut flour

0.25 tsp. salt

3 tsp baking powder, gluten-free

0.5 cup butter, unsalted

4 large eggs

0.5 tsp vanilla extract, sugar-free

12 cavity muffin tin

For the optional topping:

0.5 cup almond flour

3 tbsp. Sukrin Gold brown sugar substitute

0.25 cup butter, unsalted and melted

2 tbsp. coconut flour

0.75 tsp. ground cinnamon

Directions

Adjust your stove to heat at the temperature of 325ºF.

Cover the 12 cavities with silicone or baking cups and set to the side.

Blend the salt, cinnamon, baking powder, coconut flour, Swerve, and almond flour in a glass dish until all lumpiness is no longer present.

Combine the vanilla extract, almond milk, eggs, and butter into the mix and blend until incorporated fully.

Equally distribute to the prepped cupcake tin.

For the optional glaze, dissolve the butter in a saucepan and turn the burner off.

Combine the cinnamon, coconut flour, Sukrin Gold, and almond flour in a 2.125" round pan and evenly distribute to the top of the batter.

Heat in the stove for approximately half an hour and take out to place on the countertop.

Wait about 10 minutes before serving and enjoy!

Lemon Poppyseed Muffins

Prep 10 minutes / Cook 30 minutes/ Serves 12/ 350ºF

Difficulty: Expert

PER SERVING: Calories: 130; Protein: 4g; Net carbohydrates: 1.7g; Fat: 12g; Sugar: 0g

Ingredients

0.25 cup golden flaxseed meal

0.75 cup almond flour

0.33 cup Erythritol sweetener, granulated

2 tbsp poppy seeds

1 tbsp baking powder, gluten-free

3 large eggs

0.25 cup butter, salted and melted

2 tbsp lemon zest

0.25 cup heavy cream

25 drops Stevia liquid

1 tsp vanilla extract, sugar-free

3 tbsp lemon juice

Directions

Liquefy the butter in a 5.5" saucepan and turn the burner off.

In the meantime, prepare a muffin tin with baking cups or silicone. Set to the side.

Heat your stove to the temperature of 350ºF.

Combine the poppy seeds, Erythritol, flaxseed meal, and almond flour with a whisk until integrated.

Blend the heavy cream, eggs, and melted butter until incorporated fully.

Finally combine the lemon juice, vanilla extract, Stevia liquid, baking powder, and lemon zest into the mix and blend well.

Divide the batter equally to the prepped muffin tin and heat for approximately 20 minutes.

Place on the countertop and wait about 10 minutes before serving.

Buns

Keto hamburger buns

Prep 5 minutes / Cook 15 minutes / Serves 5/ 400ºF

Difficulty: Expert

PER SERVING: Calories: 294; Carbohydrates: 7g; Protein:14g; Fat: 25g; Fiber: 3g

Ingredients

1 ¼ cup almond flour

1 ½ cup mozzarella cheese (part skim grated)

2 oz cream cheese

1 egg (large)

2 tbsps oat fiber 500/ protein powder

1 tbsp baking powder

Directions

Using a microwave safe bowl, put the cream cheese and mozzarella cheese. Microwave the cheese for I minutes. Remove the bowl, stir and microwave again for 40 seconds to another minute.

Scrape out the cheese and place it together with the egg into a food processor. Stop when it's smooth. Add your dry ingredients, processing it till dough is formed. (It is normally very sticky) Let the dough cool.

Preheat your oven to 400ºF, placing the rack in the middle. Line your baking sheet with parchment paper and place the cheap metal plate or pan at the bottom of the oven.

Once the oven is ready, separate the dough into 5 equal portions. Apply oil on your hands (not too much) and roll the portions into balls. Place them on the parchment paper, flattening them a bit while creating a domed shape.

Put 5 or 6 ice cubes on the metal pan and place the buns inside the oven. The steam from the cubes will make the buns rise.

Bake them for about fifteen minutes. They should be done once they brown on the outside. If not, give them more minutes in the oven.

Note: Store in the fridge in an airtight container.

Paleo, Keto buns

Prep 10 minutes / Cook 45 minutes / Serves 10/ 350ºF

Difficulty: Beginner

PER SERVING: Calories: 169; Iron: 0.7mg; Calcium: 45mg; Fiber: 4g; Potassium: 50mg; Sodium: 38mg; Cholesterol: 14mg; Saturated fat: 4g; Fat

Ingredients

1 ½ cup (150g) almond meal

½ cup (60g) coconut flour

½ cup flax meal

2/3 cup psyllium husks

6 egg whites (large)

2 eggs (large)

5 tbsps sesame seeds

2 tsps. garlic powder

2 tsps. cream of tartar/ apple cider vinegar

2 tsp onion powder

1 tsp baking soda

1 tsp sea salt/ pink Himalayan

2 tbsps Erythritol (optional)

480 ml boiling water

Directions

Preheat your oven to 350ºF

Mix all your dry ingredients in a mixing bowl.

Add your egg whites and eggs. Use a hand mixer to process it till your dough becomes thick.

Add the boiling water and process until it combines.

Line your baking sheet with parchment paper.

Use a spoon to make the buns and create a dome shape.

Sprinkle the sesame seeds on the buns. Press the seeds into the buns to prevent them from falling out.

Bake for 45 minutes.

Almond Buns

Prep 10 minutes / Cook 17 minutes / Serves 3/ 350° F

Difficulty: Intermediate

PER SERVING: Calories: 373, Fat: 35 g, Protein: 10 g, Carbohydrates: 4g, Sodium: 423mg; Fiber: 2g; Sugar: 1g

Ingredients:

¾ cup almond flour

1 ½ tsps. baking powder

2 eggs, large & preferably farm-raised

1 ½ tsp Splenda

5 tbsps butter, organic & melted

Ingredients:

To make almond buns, combine almond flour, Splenda, baking powder in a large mixing bowl.

To this, add the eggs one at a time and whisk them well.

Next, spoon in the melted butter and whisk until everything comes together.

Divide the mixture into six portions and place them on a muffin top 13.75"x 10.25" pan. Spread it evenly.

Finally, bake at 350° F for 13 to 17 minutes or until the edges start to brown. Tip: keep a close watch.

Allow it to cool completely before serving.

Sesame Buns

Prep 10 minutes / Cook 45 minutes / Serves 6/ 350ºF

Difficulty: Beginner

PER SERVING: Calories: 135; Iron: 22mg; Calcium: 32mg; Fiber: 4g; Sodium: 54mg; Cholesterol: 23mg; Saturated fat: 2g; Fat Time: 25 minutes

Ingredients:

1 tsp kosher or sea salt

2 tsp baking powder

4 tbsp butter (melted)

2 cups mozzarella cheese (shredded)

3 cups almond meal or almond flour

3 big eggs

4 ounces cream cheese

dried parsley

sesame seeds

Directions:

First, preheat your oven to 400°F and use paper liners to line your muffin tin.

In a microwave-safe container, combine the cream cheese and mozzarella cheese. Place the container in the microwave and melt at intervals of 30-seconds each.

Add the eggs then stir to incorporate. Add the salt, almond meal (or flour), and baking powder then continue stirring to combine.

Form the dough into balls, place on your baking sheet, and press down slightly to flatten

Brush the top of each bun with melted butter and top with parsley and sesame seeds.

Place the baking sheet in the oven and bake the sesame buns for 10 to 12 minutes.

Low-carb coconut hamburger buns

Prep 10 minutes/ Cook 20 minutes / Serves 4/ 380ºF

Difficulty: Intermediate

PER SERVING: Calories- 218; Fat- 13.5g, Carbs- 7.2g, Dietary fiber- 3.5g, Protein- 17g.

Ingredients

½ cup coconut flour

1 ½ cups mozzarella cheese (shredded)

2 tbsps cream cheese (softened)

2 tbsps flax meal

2 eggs (large)

1 tbsp baking powder

1 tbsp sesame seeds

½ tsp salt

Directions

Preheat your oven to 380ºF.

Using a mixing bowl, whisk your flax meal, coconut flour, salt and baking soda.

In another bowl, put your cream cheese and mozzarella cheese. Microwave your cheese for 45 seconds to a minute. Stir it and microwave once more until it becomes melted.

Beat your eggs, adding into the first bowl which has the dry ingredients. Add the cheese too to the bowl. You can use your hand mixer to make the dough.

Separate the dough into four equal portions. Use these portions to make the buns and sprinkle sesame seeds. Press the seeds to prevent them from falling out.

Line the baking sheet with parchment paper and place your buns.

Bake for 20 minutes or until they brown on the outside.

Leave them to cool.

Cookies

Low-Carb Chocolate Chip Cookies

Prep 10 minutes/ Cook 12 minutes / Serves 12/ 350ºF

Difficulty: Intermediate

PER SERVING: Calories 148, Fat: 14 g, Protein: 3 g, Carbs: 3 g,

Ingredients

1.5 cups Almond Flour

½ tsp Baking Powder

¼ tsp Salt

1 cup Sugar-Free Chocolate Chips

1 stick Butter, softened

1 tsp Vanilla Extract

½ cup Swerve Granular Sweetener

1 Whole Egg

Directions

Preheat oven to 350ºF.

Cream butter and sweetener with a mixer.

Mix in the egg and vanilla extract.

Whisk together the almond flour, baking powder, and salt in a separate bowl.

Mix the dry ingredients into the wet mixture.

Fold in the chocolate chips into the dough.

Scoop the dough into a baking sheet lined with parchment. Press slightly to flatten.

Bake for 12 minutes.

Apricot and Cream Cheese Cookies

Prep 10 minutes/ Cook 12 minutes / Serves 15/ 350ºF

Difficulty: Beginner-Intermediate-Expert

PER SERVING: Calories: 122, Fat: 11 g, Protein: 4 g, Carbohydrates: 3 g, Fiber 0.9g

Ingredients:

2 cups Almond Flour

½ tsp Baking Powder

¼ tsp Salt

¼ cup Cream Cheese, softened

¼ cup Sugar-Free Apricot Preserve

¼ cup Butter, softened

1 tsp Vanilla Extract

½ cup Swerve Granular Sweetener

1 Whole Egg

Directions

Preheat oven to 350ºF

With a hand mixer, beat together the butter, cream cheese, sweetener, and apricot preserve until fluffy.

Mix in the egg and vanilla extract.

Whisk together the almond flour, baking powder, and salt in a separate bowl.

Mix the dry ingredients into the wet mixture.

Scoop the dough into a baking sheet lined with parchment. Press slightly to flatten.

Bake for 12 minutes.

Almond Butter Cookies

Prep 10 minutes/ Cook 12 minutes / Serves 12/ 350ºF

Difficulty: Intermediate

PER SERVING: Calories: 159, Fat: 14 g, Protein: 5 g, Carbs: 5 g

Ingredients:

1 cup Almond Butter

¼ cup Coconut Flour

½ cup Erythritol

¼ cup Slivered Almonds

1 Whole Egg

1 tsp Vanilla Extract

Directions

Preheat oven to 350ºF.

Mix together the almond butter, coconut flour, erythritol, vanilla, and egg in a bowl until well combined.

Fold in the slivered almonds.

Scoop the dough into a baking sheet lined with parchment. Press slightly to flatten.

Bake for 12 minutes.

Choco Hazelnut Butter Cookies

Prep 10 minutes/ Cook 12 minutes / Serves 12/ 350ºF

Difficulty: Intermediate

PER SERVING: Calories: 168, Fat: 8 g, Protein: 1 g, Protein: 7g; Carbohydrates: 2g; Sodium: 96mg; Fiber: 0g; Sugar: 1g

Ingredients

1 cup Hazelnut Butter

¼ cup Unsweetened Cocoa Powder

½ cup Erythritol

¼ cup Sugar-Free Chocolate Chips

1 Whole Egg

¼ cup Almond Milk

1 tsp Vanilla Extract

Directions

Preheat oven to 350ºF.

Mix together the hazelnut butter, cocoa powder, and erythritol in a bowl until well combined.

Stir in the egg and vanilla extract.

Add in milk a tbsp at a time.

Fold in the chocolate chips.

Scoop the dough into a baking sheet lined with parchment. Press slightly to flatten.

Bake for 12 minutes.

Banana Walnut Cookies

Prep 10 minutes/ Cook 12 minutes / Serves 12/ 350ºF

Difficulty: Beginner

PER SERVING: Calories: 112, Fat: 8 g, Saturated Fat: 1g; Protein: 3 g, Carbohydrates: 8 g; Fiber: 1g; Sugar: 1g

Ingredients

1.5 cups Almond Flour

1 cup Mashed Bananas

¼ cup Peanut Butter

¼ cup Walnuts, chopped

Directions

Preheat oven to 350ºF.

In a bowl, mix almond flour, mashed bananas, and peanut butter until well combined.

Fold in the walnuts into the dough.

Scoop the dough into a baking sheet lined with parchment. Press slightly to flatten.

Bake for 12 minutes.

Pancakes

Almond Banana Pancakes

Prep 10 minutes/ Cook 10 minutes / Serves 4

Difficulty: Beginner

PER SERVING: Calories: 235, Fat: 17 g, Saturated Fat: 3g Carbohydrates: 10 g, Protein: 11 g, Sodium: 116mg; Fiber: 3g; Sugar: 1g

Ingredients

1 Ripe Banana, mashed

4 Eggs

½ cup Almond Flour

2 tbsp Erythritol

1 tsp Baking Powder

1 tsp Ground Cinnamon

Directions

Whisk together almond flour, baking powder, and cinnamon in a bowl.

In a separate bowl, mix together mashed banana, eggs, and erythritol.

Gradually fold in the dry ingredients into the wet mixture.

Preheat a skillet and coat with non-stick spray.

Ladle in the batter and cook for 1-2 minutes per side.

Jalapeno and Cream Cheese Pancakes

Prep 5 minutes/ Cook 10 minutes/ Serves 4

Difficulty: Intermediate

PER SERVING: Calories: 230, Fat: 19 g, Saturated Fat: 3g; Protein: 10 g, Carbs: 2 g, Fiber: 3g; Sugar: 1g

Ingredients

½ cup Cream Cheese

4 Eggs

½ cup Almond Flour

1 tbsp Minced Jalapenos

Directions

Mix all ingredients in a blender.

Preheat a skillet and coat with non-stick spray.

Ladle in the batter and cook for 1-2 minutes per side.

Coconut Chia Pancakes

Prep 5 minutes/ Cook 10 minutes/ Serves 4

Difficulty: Beginner

PER SERVING: Calories: 333, Fat: 30 g, Protein: 10 g, Carbohydrates: 6 g, Sodium: 106mg; Fiber: 1g; Sugar: 2g

Ingredients

½ cup Coconut Flour

4 Eggs

1 cup Coconut Milk

1 tsp Psyllium Husk

½ tsp Baking Powder

1 tbsp Coconut Oil

1 tbsp Chia Seeds

Directions

Mix all ingredients in a blender.

Preheat a skillet and coat with non-stick spray.

Ladle in the batter and cook for 1-2 minutes per side.

Keto Blueberry Pancakes

Prep 10 minutes/ Cook 10 minutes/ Serves 4

Difficulty: Beginner

PER SERVING: Calories: 287, Fat: 25 g, Saturated Fat: 5g; Protein: 11 g, Carbohydrates: 4 g; Fiber: 0g; Sugar: 3g

Ingredients

½ cup Cream Cheese

4 Eggs

2 tbsp Melted Butter

½ cup Almond Flour

2 tbsp Erythritol

1 tsp Baking Powder

¼ tsp Salt

¼ cup Fresh Blueberries

Directions

Whisk together almond flour, baking powder, and salt in a bowl.

In a separate bowl, mix together cream cheese, eggs, butter, and erythritol.

Gradually stir in the dry ingredients into the wet mixture.

Fold in the blueberries.

Preheat a skillet and coat with non-stick spray.

Ladle in the batter and cook for 1-2 minutes per side.

Spiced Pumpkin Pancakes

Prep 10 minutes/ Cook 10 minutes/ Serves 4

Difficulty: Intermediate

PER SERVING: Calories: 280, Fat: 23 g, Saturated Fat: 5g; Protein: 12 g, Carbs: 9 g, Fiber: 3g; Sugar: 2g

Ingredients

1 cup Almond Flour

1 tbsp Pumpkin Pie Spice

½ tsp Baking Powder

2 tbsp Erythritol

3 Eggs

¼ cup Pumpkin Puree

¼ cup Coconut Milk

Directions

Mix all ingredients in a blender.

Preheat a skillet and coat with non-stick spray.

Ladle in the batter and cook for 1-2 minutes per side.

Low-Carb Red Velvet Pancakes

Prep 5 minutes/ Cook 10 minutes/ Serves 4

Difficulty: Expert

PER SERVING: Calories: 339, Fat: 29 g, Saturated Fat: 9g; Protein: 13 g, Carbohydrates: 5 g, Fiber: 1g; Sugar: 2g

Ingredients

½ cup Cream Cheese

4 Eggs

2 tbsp Butter, melted

½ cup Almond Flour

1 tbsp Unsweetened Cocoa Powder

2 tbsp Erythritol

1 tsp Vanilla Extract

½ tsp Red Food Coloring

Directions

Mix all ingredients in a blender.

Preheat a skillet and coat with non-stick spray.

Ladle in the batter and cook for 1-2 minutes per side.

Citrus and Ricotta Pancakes

Prep 5 minutes/ Cook 10/ minutes Serves 4

Difficulty: Intermediate

PER SERVING: Calories:256, Fat: 20 g, Saturated Fat: 1g; Protein: 15 g, Carbohydrates: 5 g, Fiber: 1g; Sugar: 1g

Ingredients

½ cup Ricotta Cheese

4 Eggs

½ cup Almond Flour

1 tsp Orange Zest

1 tsp Vanilla Extract

Directions

Mix all ingredients in a blender.

Preheat a skillet and coat with non-stick spray.

Ladle in the batter and cook for 1-2 minutes per side.

Keto Bacon and Cheese Pancakes

Prep 10 minutes / Cook 10 minutes / Serves 4

Difficulty: Intermediate

PER SERVING: Calories: 290, Fat: 22 g, Protein: 17 g, Carbohydrates: 6 g, Sodium: 79mg; Fiber: 2g; Sugar: 3g

Ingredients

½ cup Shredded Cheddar

4 Eggs, separated

½ cup Almond Flour

½ tsp Cream of Tartar

¼ tsp Salt

¼ cup Bacon Bits

1 tbsp Chopped Chives

Directions

Whisk the egg whites and cream of tartar until soft peaks from.

Sift in the almond flour and salt.

Fold in the cheddar, bacon, and chives.

Lightly coat a 10" non-stick pan with cooking spray.

Ladle the batter in and cook for 1-2 minutes per side.

Croissants

French Croissant

Prep 40 minutes / Cook 15 minutes / Serves 12

Difficulty: Expert

PER SERVING: Calories: 196, Fat: 22 g, Protein: 13.4 g, Carbohydrates: 6 g, Sodium: 304mg; Fiber: 0.6g; Sugar: 2g

Ingredients:

1.75 cups all-purpose flour

0.75 cup milk, warm

1 tsp white sugar

2 tsp white sugar

1.5 tsp salt

¾ cup chilled unsalted butter

3 tbsp warm water

2 tbsp vegetable oil

1.5 tsp dry yeast

1 tbsp water

1 egg

Directions:

Mix water, yeast and 1 tsp sugar and set aside until it becomes creamy.

Add flour to a mixing bowl and add milk salt and sugar. Combine with the yeast mixture and thoroughly mix. Set aside for about 3 hours to let it rise.

Apply butter till it is pliable. Pat the dough on a rectangle which is 14"x8" and smear butter on 2/3 and leave a 1/3 margin. Fold the 1/3 which is not buttered over the third at the center and the 1/3 top third which is buttered over that. Turn right and roll it on the triangle and fold thrice. Drizzle some flour and put in plastic bag

Roll dough on the rectangle and cut crosswise into two. Shape one of the two while the other is chilling. Cut into squares of 5x5" and half diagonally cut the squares and elongate every triangle by rolling.

Put on a baking sheet and let them rise.

Mix egg, water in a different bowl and glaze the croissant. Bake for 15 minutes. Cool before serving.

Pumpkin Pie Baked Croissants

Prep 10 minutes / Cook 20 minutes / Serves 6

Difficulty: Expert

PER SERVING: Calories: 110, Fat: 10 g, Protein: 10 g, Carbohydrates: 6g, Sodium: 244mg; Fiber: 0.6g; Sugar: 2g

Ingredients:

1 cup unsalted butter (at room temperature)

½ cup granulated sugar

1 cup pureed pumpkin

1 egg

1 tbsp. all-purpose flour

2 tsp vanilla essence

2 tsp pumpkin pie spice

Pinch kosher salt

6 large bakery croissants (halved lengthwise)

Confectioner's sugar (for dusting)

Directions:

Preheat the main oven to 350°F. Line a baking sheet with parchment.

Beat together the butter and granulated sugar until fluffy.

Beat in the pureed pumpkin, egg, all-purpose flour, vanilla essence, pie spice, and kosher salt for 2-3 minutes until super light.

Spread 1-2 tbsp. of the mixture into each sliced croissant.

Arrange the filled croissants on a baking sheet. Spread any remaining pumpkin mixture on top of the croissants.

Place in the oven and bake for 20 minutes.

Allow to cool a little before dusting with confectioner's sugar and serving warm.

Quick Croissant

Prep 20 minutes / Cook 25 minutes / Serves 8/ 450°F

Difficulty: Expert

PER SERVING: Calories: 290, Fat: 22 g, Protein: 5.5g, Carbohydrates: 5g, Sodium: 267mg; Fiber: 1.5g; Sugar: 5.4g

Ingredients:

2 cups flour

1 tbsp milk

½ tsp salt

½ cup warm milk

25g fresh yeast

1 egg yolk

3 tbsp sugar

Egg Wash

1.25 sticks unsalted butter, diced

Directions

Put fresh yeast in a bowl. Stir in sugar until it dissolves. Pour in the milk and let it cool.

In a bowl, mix salt and flour and then add butter. Combine using a fork to form crumbles.

Pour in the yeast mixture and mix to form dough. Wrap the butter in a plastic so as to keep it in pea-size pieces and put in a freezer for half an hour.

Dust the rolling pin and the working surface and the roll the dough into rectangular shape.

Fold the widths of the dough to the center. Twist the dough for a ¼ turn and roll it and fold the edges.

Turn the dough upside down and repeat the folding.

Cover the dough in a plastic and put in the refrigerator for a few hours.

Roll dough on a surface drizzled with flour into a four-sided shape (rectangle). Cut the dough using a knife into triangles.

Make a slit on each triangle's center and stretch the tip and corners roll then to form a croissant.

Put the croissants on the parchment paper-lined baking sheet and cover and allow 2 hours to rise.

Preheat oven to 450°F. use the egg wash to brush the croissants.

Bake for 10 minutes and lower the temperature to 375°F and bake for 15 more minutes. Put on a rack to cool and serve.

Campfire Croissants

Prep 10 minutes / Cook 5 minutes / Serves 6

Difficulty: Intermediate

PER SERVING: Calories: 211, Fat: 13 g, Protein: 9 g, Carbohydrates: 5.6 g, Sodium: 342mg; Fiber: 2g; Sugar: 4g

Ingredients:

2 tsp brown sugar

2 tsp cinnamon

2 tsp nutmeg

4 tbsp. salted butter (melted)

6 large croissants (halved lengthwise)

18 large marshmallows

6 ounces semisweet chocolate squares

Directions:

Preheat your grill for direct grilling on a moderately high heat.

Combine the sugar, cinnamon, and nutmeg in a small dish.

Brush each croissant half with melted butter on the cut-sides only. Sprinkle each croissant half with the spiced sugar.

Take 6 skewers and slide 3 marshmallows onto each.

Toast each croissant half, buttered side down, for 60 seconds. Take off the grill and divide the chocolate squares equally among the bottom halves.

Grill the marshmallows for 90 seconds, turning once. Slide 3 marshmallows onto each chocolatey croissant base.

Sandwich together with the toasted croissant tops.

Enjoy straight away!

Almond Croissant Brunch Bake

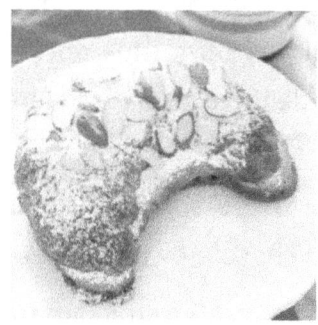

Prep 10 minutes/ Cook 45 minutes / Serves 6

Difficulty: Expert

PER SERVING: Calories: 135, Fat: 11 g, Saturated Fat: 2g Carbohydrates: 5 g, Protein: 10 g, Sodium: 201mg; Fiber: 2g; Sugar: 2g

Ingredients:

2 medium eggs

cup granulated sugar

2 cups whole milk

tsp kosher salt

4 large croissants (torn into pieces)

3 tbsp. flaked almonds

Butter (for greasing)

Directions:

Preheat the main oven to 300 degrees F. Grease a (1½-2 quart) shallow baking dish.

Whisk together the eggs, granulated sugar, whole milk, and kosher salt until well combined.

Toss the torn croissants in the liquid until coated. Set aside to soak for 7-9 minutes.

Transfer the mixture to the baking dish and use a spatula to smooth down the surface. Scatter with the flaked almonds.

Place in the oven and bake for approximately 45 minutes, until the custard has set.

Allow to stand for several minutes before slicing and serving.

Pizza

Cauliflower Pizza Crust

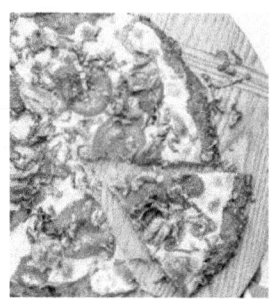

Prep 10 minutes/ Cook 35 minutes/ Serves 8/ 405ºF

Difficulty: Expert

PER SERVING: Calories: 278; Fat: 21g; Saturated Fat: 2g; Protein: 11g; Carbohydrates: 5g; Sodium: 102mg; Fiber: 1g; Sugar: 3g

Ingredients

0.5 tsp salt

16 oz. cauliflower florets

1 large egg

1.5 tbsp coconut flour

3 tsp avocado oil

0.5 tsp Italian seasoning

1 tsp coconut oil

Directions

Set your oven to heat at the temperature of 405ºF.

Pulse the cauliflower in a food blender for approximately 60 seconds until it is a crumbly consistency.

Heat the coconut oil and cauliflower in a 9"x 9" frypan for approximately 5 minutes as it becomes tender.

Transfer the cauliflower to a kitchen towel and twist to eliminate the extra water. Repeat this step as many times as necessary to make sure the moisture has been eliminated.

Prepare your 10" pizza pan or flat sheet with a section of baking lining and set to the side.

In a glass dish, blend the riced cauliflower, salt, egg, coconut flour, avocado oil, and Italian seasoning and integrate until it thickens.

Flatten the dough onto the prepped pan to no less than a quarter inch.

Heat for 25 minutes if then and up to half an hour if thicker.

Complete with your favorite toppings and finish in the stove for another 5 minutes. Enjoy!

Mozzarella Pizza Crust

Prep 7 minutes/ Cook 25 minutes/ Serves 8/ 350ºF

Difficulty: Intermediate

PER SERVING: Calories: 190, Carbohydrates: 1.4 g, Fat: 6 g, Saturated Fat: 1g; Fiber: 2g Sugar: 2g

Ingredients

1.5 cups mozzarella cheese, shredded

0.75 cup almond flour

1 whole egg

2 tbsp cream cheese, full-fat

0.25 tsp salt

Directions

Set your stove to heat at the temperature of 350ºF.

Use a microwave-safe dish to nuke the almond flour, mozzarella, and cream cheese for approximately 60 seconds until liquefied.

Toss the cheese and heat for an additional half minute.

Blend the salt and egg into the cheese for about half a minute.

Place a section of baking lining on the counter and transfer the dough to the middle. Use another section of baking lining to place on top.

Flatten to no less than a quarter of an inch. Separate the top baking lining and transfer to 10" pan.

Heat for approximately 13 minutes until turning golden.

Layer with your toppings of choice and heat for about 5 minutes.

Serve hot and enjoy!

Zucchini Pizza Crust

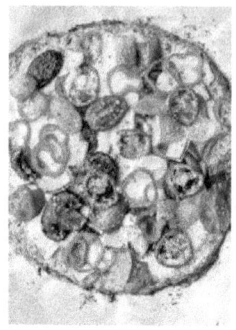

Prep 15 minutes/ Cook 45minutes/ Serves 8/ 400ºF

Difficulty: Intermediate

PER SERVING: Calories: 127, Protein: 7g, Fat: 8 g, Saturated Fat: 2g; Carbohydrates: 4 g, Fiber: 1g; Sugar: 2g

Ingredients

4 cups zucchini, shredded

1 cup almond flour

2.75 tbsp coconut flour

4 tbsp nutritional yeast

1.33 tbsp Italian seasoning

0.75 tsp salt

3 large eggs

Directions

Adjust the temperature of your stove to heat at 400ºF.

Cover a 12.75" pan with a layer of baking lining and set to the side.

Use a kitchen grater to shred the zucchini using the largest holes available.

Transfer to a kitchen towel and wring to release all excess moisture.

In a glass dish, blend the coconut flour, zucchini, salt, Italian seasoning, nutritional yeast, eggs, and almond flour until integrated and thickened.

Distribute to the prepped sheet and flatten to no less than quarter an inch by hand.

Heat for the duration of 20 minutes. Turn the crust over and warm for another 10 minutes.

Layer with your preferred toppings and heat for another 13 minutes.

Wait about 10 minutes before slicing and serving. Enjoy!

Fat Head Pizza Dough - Egg & Gluten-Free

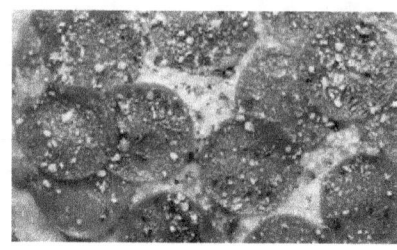

Prep 15 minutes/Cook 30minutes/ Serves 8/ 425ºF

Difficulty: Expert

PER SERVING: Calories: 161; Fat: 13g; Saturated Fat: 1g; Carbohydrates: 2g; Protein: 9g; Sodium: 132mg; Fiber: 0g; Sugar: 2g

Ingredients

8 oz. Mozzarella cheese slices full fat

2 tbsp grated parmesan cheese

2 tbsp full-fat cream cheese

1/3 cup almond flour

½ tsp garlic powder

½ tsp salt

2 tbsp whole psyllium husks either whole or ground

Directions

Finely chop and place the mozzarella in a microwaveable container. Cook until melted. (This took about 1.5 minutes.)

Let the cheese cool slightly. Mix with the cream cheese, almond flour, parmesan cheese, garlic powder, and salt. (Knead in with your hands.)

Add the psyllium and shape the dough into a ball and then roll out as flat as you can on parchment paper, pizza stone, or a silicone mat.

Shape the dough as needed and bake at 425ºF for about 15-20 minutes.

Flip the crust and bake for about 5 more minutes until browned.

Add the sauce, cheese, and other toppings. Bake for about five more minutes.

Keto Pizza Pockets

Prep 5minutes/ Cook 7 minutes/ Serves 4

Difficulty: Beginner

PER SERVING: Calories: 293; Fat: 3.9g; Saturated Fat: 2g; Protein: 15.6g; Carbohydrates: 1.8g; Sodium: 96mg; Fiber: 0g; Sugar: 1g

Ingredients

1 ¾ cups pre-shredded/grated cheese mozzarella

¾ cup almond flour

2 tbsp full-fat cream cheese

1 medium egg

1 pinch salt

Directions

Mix the shredded cheese, cream cheese, and almond flour in a microwaveable bowl. Microwave using high power for one minute.

Stir and continue cooking on high for another 30 seconds.

Whisk the egg and salt and mix gently with the rest of the fixings.

Roll the dough between two sheets of parchment baking paper. (Don't roll as thin as a thin pizza crust so it can hold the chosen fillings.)

Discard the top baking paper. Slice the dough into squares (the same size as your toasted sandwich maker).

Place one square on the bottom of the sandwich maker, add your choice of fillings.

Place another square of dough on the top and press the lid of the sandwich maker down.

Cook until they're golden brown or about three to five minutes.

Low-Carb Cauliflower Pizza Crust

Prep 5 minutes/ Cook 7 minutes/ Serves 4

Difficulty: Intermediate

PER SERVING: Calories: 147; Fat: 10g; Saturated Fat: 2g; Protein: 14g; Carbohydrates: 1g; Sodium: 67mg; Fiber: 0g; Sugar: 0g

Ingredients:

1 cup Riced cauliflower - cooked

1 Egg

Spices - optional - ex. parsley, fennel, oregano, etc.

Directions:

Set the oven temperature setting at 450º Fahrenheit.

Spray a 12 " pizza pan with a spritz of cooking oil spray.

Mix the cauliflower, egg, and mozzarella. Press onto the pie plate. Sprinkle with the spices and bake for 12 to 15 minutes. Remove and add the sauce, cheese, and toppings.

Put the pizza under the high-heat broiler to melt the cheese.

Stovetop Pizza Crust

Prep 15 minutes/ Cook 30 minutes/ Serves 6/ 350° F

Difficulty: Intermediate

PER SERVING: Calories: 118; Fat: 9g; Saturated Fat: 1g; Protein: 5.6g; Carbohydrates: 1.8g; Sodium: 103mg; Fiber: 0g; Sugar: 4g

Ingredient:

1 cup Almond flour

3 tbsp. Coconut flour

2 tsp. Xanthan gum

1 tsp.Bak. powder

¼ tsp Kosher salt

2 tsp. Apple cider vinegar

1 Egg, lightly beaten

5 tsp. Water

Directions:

Measure out and add the xanthan gum, almond flour, baking powder, coconut flour, and salt to a food processor. Pulse well to fully combine.

With the processor running, add the vinegar, the egg, and water. Add just enough for it to come together into a ball.

Wrap the dough in plastic wrap and knead it through the plastic for a minute or two. Allow the dough to rest for 10 minutes at room temperature for up to five days in the fridge.

If cooking on the stovetop, warm up the skillet using the med-high temperature while your dough rests. For the oven; heat up the baking tray, pizza stone, or skillet to reach 350° Fahrenheit.

Roll out the dough between two sheets of parchment paper. Fold over the edges.

Prepare the pizza crust in the preheated skillet, top-side down first, until blistered (about 2 min.).

Reduce the heat to med-low. Flip the pizza crust, and add the toppings of choice. Cover with a lid.

When ready, serve immediately for best results.

You can store the dough in the refrigerator for approximately five days.

Rolls

Low-carb dinner rolls

Prep 10 minutes/ Cook 10 minutes/ Serves 6/ 350° F

Difficulty: Intermediate

PER SERVING: Calories: 218; Fat: 18g; Saturated Fat: 5g; Protein: 10.7g; Carbohydrates: 5.6g; Sodium: 103mg; Fiber: 3.3g; Sugar: 3g

Ingredients

1 cup almond flour

¼ cup flaxseed (ground)

1 cup Mozzarella (shredded)

1 oz cream cheese

½ tsp baking soda

1 egg

Directions:

Preheat your oven to 400°F.

Using a microwave-safe mixing bowl, put both the mozzarella and cream cheese. Microwave it for one minute. Stir them till they become smooth.

Add eggs in the bowl and stir till they mix well.

In another clean bowl, put your flaxseed, almond flour and baking soda and mix the dry ingredients.

Pour your egg and cheese mix into the bowl with dry ingredients. Use your hand mixer or hands to make dough by kneading.

Slightly wet your hands with coconut oil or olive oil and roll your dough to six balls.

Top them with sesame seeds and place them on the parchment paper.

Bake them for 10 minutes. A golden brown look will indicate that they are done.

Leave them to cool.

Low-carb clover rolls

Prep 10 minutes/ Cook 20 minutes/ Serves 8/ 350° F

Difficulty: Intermediate

PER SERVING: Calories: 283; Fat: 18g; Saturated Fat: 21g; Protein: 17g; Carbohydrates: 6g; Sodium: 103mg; Fiber: 2g; Sugar: 1g

Ingredients

1/3 cup coconut flour or 1 1/3 cup almond flour

1 ½ cup mozzarella cheese (shredded)

1 ½ tsp baking powder

¼ cup parmesan cheese (grated)

2 ounces cream cheese

2 eggs (large)

Directions:

Preheat your oven to 350°F.

Put your almond flour and baking powder in a clean bowl and mix.

Using another bowl, put your Mozzarella and cream cheese and microwave for a minute. Stir it well after it melts.

Add eggs to the cheese and stir.

Add the egg-cheese mix to the bowl with dry ingredients and mix thoroughly.

Wet your hands and knead dough into a sticky ball.

Put the dough ball on the parchment paper and slice into fourths.

Slice each fourth or quarter into 6 smaller portions.

Roll each small portion into balls.

Roll the balls into the parmesan cheese light for them to coat it.

Grease your 13.75" x 10.5" muffin pan and place 3 dough balls in each cup of the pan.

Keto bread rolls

Prep 10 minutes/ Cook 20 minutes/ Serves 8/ 350° F

Difficulty: Beginner

PER SERVING: Calories: 216; Fat: 16g; Saturated Fat: 4g; Protein: 11g; Carbohydrates: 6g; Sodium: 183mg; Fiber: 2g; Sugar: 1g

Ingredients

1 1/3 cups almond flour

1 ½ cups shredded mozzarella cheese (part skim)

2 oz cream cheese (full fat)

1 ½ tbsp baking powder (aluminum free)

2 tbsps. coconut flour

3 eggs (large)

Directions:

Preheat your oven to 350° F

In a clean bowl, put almond flour, coconut flour and baking powder. Mix well and set it aside.

Using a microwave-safe bowl, put the cream cheese and mozzarella in it and microwave for 30 seconds. Remove the bowl, stir and microwave again for 30 seconds. This should go on until the cheese has entirely melted.

Using a food processor add the cheese, the eggs and flour mix. Process at high speed for uniformity of the dough. (It is normally sticky.)

Knead the dough into a dough ball and separate it into 8 equal pieces. Slightly wet your hands with oil for this step.

Roll each piece with your palms to form a ball and place each ball on the baking sheet. (should be 2 inches apart)

In a bowl, add the remaining egg and whisk. Brush the egg wash on the rolls.

Bake for 20 minutes or until they are golden brown.

Note: The cheese hardens the rolls thus they should be eaten when hot. Microwave them to make soft once they cool.

Keto coconut bread rolls

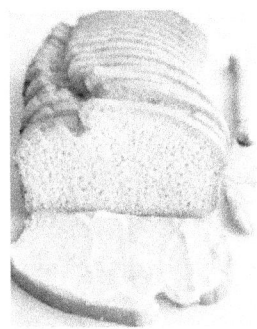

Prep 10 minutes/ Cook 30 minutes/ Serves 6/ 350° F

Difficulty: Intermediate

PER SERVING: Calories: 172; Fat: 10g; Saturated Fat: 2g; Protein: 10.7g; Carbohydrates: 14g; Sodium: 100mg; Fiber: 9g; Sugar: 1g

Ingredients

½ cup coconut flour

4 tbsps. flaxseed (ground)

2 tbsps. coconut oil

2 tbsps. psyllium husk (powder)

1 tbsp baking powder

1 tbsp apple cider vinegar

¼ cup boiling water

½ tsp salt

2 egg whites

2 eggs (medium size)

Directions:

Preheat your oven to 350°F.

In a mixing bowl, put all your dry ingredients and mix thoroughly. (coconut flour, flaxseed flour, baking powder, psyllium husk powder, salt)

Add eggs and the coconut oil. Blend the ingredients till it resembles breadcrumbs. Pour the apple cider vinegar and mix.

Add the boiling water in bits. (you don't need to use the entire amount) Stir for it to combine well with the mixture.

Line your baking tray with baking paper.

Make 6 divisions of the dough and roll them into balls with your hands.

Place the dough balls on the baking paper.

Bake them for 30 minutes or upon turning to golden brown.

Low carb bread rolls (without eggs)

Prep 15 minutes/ Cook 40 minutes/ Serves 6/ 350° F

Difficulty: Intermediate

PER SERVING: Calories: 230; Fat: 18g; Saturated Fat: 5g; Protein: 6.2g; Carbohydrates: 13.9g; Sodium: 132mg; Fiber: 9.2g; Sugar: 1.9g

Ingredients

¼ cup coconut flour

1 ¼ cup almond flour

¼ cup psyllium husk (ground)

1 cup hot water

1 tbsp olive oil

2 tsp apple cider vinegar

2 tsps. baking powder

½ tsp salt

2 tbsps. sesame seeds (optional)

Directions:

Preheat your oven to 375°F.

Add all your dry ingredients in a bowl. (Coconut flour, almond flour, psyllium powder, baking powder, salt)

Pour the olive oil and apple cider vinegar in the hot water and stir. Thereafter, pour the mix in the bowl and combine thoroughly for a minute. The flour will absorb the water forming the dough. The dough will be soft and sticky. Leave it for 10 minutes for the water mixture to be well absorbed.

Separate the dough into 6 equal portions. Form 6 dough balls as a result.

Line your baking tray with parchment paper.

Place the balls on the baking tray and sprinkle sesame seeds on top. Press the seeds into the dough to prevent falling out.

Bake for 40 minutes at 375OF at the lower section of the oven for the first 30 minutes. Switch them to the top section for the remaining period.

Remove from the oven and let them cool.

Conclusion

These breads are made using the normal ingredients you can find locally, so there's no need to have to order anything, or have to go to any specialty stores for any of them. With these breads, you can enjoy the same meals you used to enjoy, but stay on track with your diet as much as you want.

Lose the weight you want to lose, feel great, and still get to indulge in that piping hot piece of bread every now and then. Spread on your favorite topping, and your bread craving will be satisfied.

I hope the recipes in this book were able to inspire you to take your own baking to the next level. As you can see by each of these, you can alter and modify a variety of things to give them that custom spin you need from time to time.

Thanks for downloading this book. It's my firm belief that it has provided you with all the answers to your questions

Part 2

Introduction

Hot and fresh homemade bread baking, which publishes a delightful fragrance, will become your pride in a family dinner or dinner. Simple and clear instructions will make the process of making dough and baking bread simple and exciting. Recipes describe the entire cooking process, and so you do not have to think about how to bake bread fast and make it tasty and fragrant. Enjoy the cooking of homemade bread.

Custard yeast dough for pies

Ingredients:

- 3 tablespoons flour
- 1 teaspoon of salt
- 1 tablespoon sugar
- 3 tablespoons vegetable oil
- 150 ml of steep boiling water
- 250 ml of water
- 500 g of flour
- 1 pack of dry yeast

Preparation:

In the dishes pour sugar, salt, flour; pour the vegetable oil and mix. 150 ml of water to bring to a boil. Pour boiling water over the mixture and mix with a spoon until a uniform mixture.

To the resulting mixture, pour another 250 ml of water at room temperature, pour in flour and dry yeast. Knead smooth dough in any convenient and affordable way, namely, hands, mixer or bakery. Set the climb for an hour and a half, during this time, crumble up the dough.

During the same time, you can prepare any desired stuffing. Ripen the dough into small juices, form pies and fry in vegetable oil.

Focaccia with filling

Ingredients:

- 500 g of flour
- 1.5 teaspoons of salt
- 8 g dry yeast
- 200 g of warm water
- 200 g of Suluguni cheese
- Dill
- Basil
- Green onion
- Olive oil
- Coarse sea salt

Preparation:

Mix the flour with salt and yeast. In the middle, make a hole and pour in warm water. Knead the dough for 10 minutes. Roll into a bowl, grease with olive oil, cover with a towel and leave in a warm place for 1 hour. After the dough has doubled in volume, mash it and divide it into 4 parts. Roll each part into a rectangle.

Grate the cheese on a small grater, cut the greens. Put the mixed greens and cheese into two rectangles. Cover each of them with the second part of the test. The edges must be carefully worn. Transfer focaccia to a baking sheet, grease with olive oil, sprinkle with sea salt and let stand for another 30 minutes.

Bake in a preheated 180 degree oven for 25 minutes.

Ciabatta

Ingredients:

- Mineral water with gas - 250 ml
- Wheat flour - 250 g
- Salt -1 teaspoon without top
- Yeast - 1 teaspoon without top

Preparation:

The dough is kneaded immediately without any opaque's, kneaded better by the combine, until the dough begins to wind on the blades.

It takes about an hour to melt, it must be very bubbly, and it all depends on the air temperature. Dough neatly put on a table, abundantly sprinkled with flour, it, as it should lie on the table, sprinkle a little flour and curl it up - mentally divide the entire layer into three parts, wrap first one piece, then wrap it with the other. In general, fold three times. Put to dissolve.

Put the bread in a well-heated oven to 250 degrees. Bake for 30 minutes; reduce the temperature to 220 degrees and another 30 minutes. The readiness of the ciabatta is determined by knocking. If you knock on the bottom of the sound will be empty. You will know exactly when you will knock, if the sound is not empty; leave it in the oven for a few more minutes.

Bread on kefir, without yeast

Ingredients:

- Kefir 1 glass
- Wheat flour about 2.5 cups
- Soda 1 teaspoon
- Salt 1 teaspoon
- Sugar a little bit
- Cumin 0.5 - 1 teaspoon
- Spices or nuts, dried fruits

Preparation:

Mix in the bowl all the dry ingredients and pour them into kefir. Stir, first with a spoon, then with a hand. The dough turns thick, soft, slightly sticking to the hands. We form a loaf from the resulting dough, in the form of a deco; we make cuts, in order to make the dough better.

In a preheated oven to 200 degrees, place our bread, sprinkled with flour, to form a crusty crust. Bake for 25 to 30 minutes. We check the bread readiness with a wooden toothpick; it must leave the bread dry and clean.

Lithuanian Homemade bread

Ingredients:

- 1 cup whole rye flour
- 1 glass of warm water
- 1 cup of sourdough
- 2 cups whole rye flour
- 0.5 glasses of warm water
- 1 cup whole rye flour
- 1 cup of wheat flour
- 1 tablespoon cumin
- 3 tablespoons sugar
- 1 tablespoon of natural honey
- 2 teaspoons of salt
- 0.5 glasses of warm water

Preparation:

Mix the flour with water until the consistency of thick sour cream. Density can be regulated by additional water addition. The resulting mass is put in a glass jar, cover with a linen towel. Leave at room temperature for 72 hours. Every day, the mass is easy to mix.

In the starter, add flour and mix to a thick, sticky state. Add water for ease of mixing. The resulting mass is covered and put for fermentation for 12 hours. At the end of fermentation, the mass should become a little bit lighter, full of bubbles and grow approximately twice.

Mix all the ingredients and knead the dough. Form bread, put in a form, made with baking paper. Leave to rise for 3 hours in a warm place. Bake in preheated to 250 degrees oven for 15 minutes; then lowering the heat to 200 degrees for about 30 minutes. Already baked bread is advised to sprinkle a little water. Bread cover with a towel and leave until completely cooled.

Wheat-rye bread

Ingredients:

- Wheat Flour - 250 g
- Rye flour - 200 g
- Vegetable oil - 2 tablespoons
- Sugar - 1,5 tablespoons
- Milk powder - 1,5 tablespoons
- Yeast dry - 2 teaspoons
- Apple vinegar - 2 tablespoons
- Salt - 1,5 teaspoons
- Water - 300 ml

Preparation:

We load the ingredients according to the instructions of your bread maker, at first dry, and then add liquid. Insert a spatula for rye bread.

Set the mode to rye. The preparation of dough and baking bread takes 3.5 hours. Cool on the grate.

Carrot and sour cream

Ingredients:

- 250-300 g of flour
- 100 g of margarine
- 1 piece egg
- 2 tablespoons sour cream
- 1 piece of carrots
- 0.5 teaspoon soda
- Salt

Preparation:

Carrots, clean, grate on a fine grater. Beat up sour cream with egg, combine with carrots. Add the melted margarine, flour, baking powder, salt to this mixture. Knead soft dough, cover with a napkin and put into the refrigerator for 20-30 minutes. The dough is rolled out 0.5 cm thick, cut out with a mold of puff, and bake for 15-20 minutes at 180 degrees.

Bread Armenian festive

Ingredients:

- 1 kg of wheat flour
- 200 g melted butter
- 350 ml of milk
- 150 g of sugar
- 2 eggs
- 0.5 teaspoon of salt
- 25 g fresh yeast
- 1 yolk
- 50 g of any nuts

Preparation:

Dilute yeast in warm milk with 1 tablespoon of sugar, leave for 5 minutes. Eggs grind with sugar, pour to the milk, mix, pour in flour and salt. Pour the melted butter and knead the dough soft, with a lightly sticking dough. Cover the dough, leave for 2 hours in a warm place, during this time, double fold.

Ready to put the dough on the floured desktop, knead and divide into 4-5 parts, from each roll out a round cake 2 x 3 cm thick or braid the pigtail.

Place on a floured baking sheet and leave for proofing for 30 minutes. Lubricate the flat cakes with yolk and sprinkle with finely chopped nuts and bake in a preheated oven for 180 minutes 30 minutes.

Indian bread "Puri"

Ingredients:

- Flour 450 g
- Sunflower oil 1 tablespoon
- Salt
- Warm water 300ml

Preparation:

Flour sift in a deep bowl, add butter 1 tablespoon, salt, and then pour over a little warm water knead the dough. The dough turns out soft, warm, elastic.

Pour flour on the work surface, lay out the dough, roll out, cut into portions and give any shape you want, you can use a rolling pin, or you can simply use your hands. Fry in a lot of lean oil, over medium heat, until golden.

Fladenbrot

Ingredients:

- 500 g of flour
- 375 ml of water
- 8 g dry yeast
- 10 g of salt
- 20g of sugar
- Seeds of black cumin for sprinkling

Preparation:

Knead the yeast dough by mixing all the ingredients into elastic soft dough. Give the test twice. Form a cake from the dough. With a sharp knife, make cuts in the form of cells. Having sprinkled a cake with water sprinkle it with seeds of black cumin or sesame. Put in an oven heated to 180 degrees and bake for 25-30 minutes.

Buckwheat bread

Ingredients:

- Water 270 g
- Grouts of buckwheat 90 g
- Wheat flour 200-210 g
- Yeast, fresh 10 g
- Salt 1 teaspoon
- Sugar 2 teaspoons

Preparation:

Buckwheat grouts rude. In general, buckwheat is a good fit, but if it does not, then grinds shortly in a coffee grinder, so that the grains are partially crushed. Pour hot water, add salt, sugar.

When the mass cools down to a warm state, and buckwheat flourishes, wheat flour, ground with yeast to crumbs, and knead soft dough. Cover, put in a warm place to fit well.

Approach the dough with your hands in a rectangle. Roll a loose loaf. Put in the form. On the surface of the roll scissors make a notch. Cover with a pack and let go as warm as possible. Bake bread at 195 degrees for 30-35 minutes. With the finished bread, the crust makes a dull sound when tapping. Bread cover, cool.

Fresh delicious bread bakery

Ingredients:

- Half a glass of warm water
- 1 egg
- 2 tablespoons vegetable oil
- 1 with top tablespoons sugar
- Slightly less than a teaspoon of salt
- 20 g fresh yeast
- 3 cups flour

Preparation:

In the bowl mixer pour water; add egg, sugar, vegetable oil, yeast. Mix. Gradually sprinkle flour, knead the dough. When half of the flour is poured, add salt. Dough well kneads.

Put on a proofing for 2 hours. Put the parchment in parchment. Make buns out of the dough. Put in a warm place for a proofing for 30 minutes. Heat the oven to 210 degrees. Lubricate the buns with milk.

You can sprinkle with sesame seeds, poppy seeds. Put a container of boiling water on the bottom of the oven. Bake for 10 minutes. Then remove the container and bake for another 5-6 minutes.

Cheese "bread"

Ingredients:

- Eggs - 2 pieces
- Milk - 225 ml
- Vegetable oil - 3 tablespoons
- Flour 270 g
- Baking Powder - 2 teaspoons
- Sugar - 1 teaspoon
- Salt 0.5 teaspoon
- Grated cheese 220 g
- Dry mustard -1 teaspoon spoon

Preparation:

Mix eggs with milk and lightly whip with whisk. Separately sift the flour with salt, sugar, baking powder and mustard. Combine both mixtures, and add grated cheese, stir well. Put into a mold and bake at 170 degrees for 30-40 minutes. Cool it down.

Steamed bread with balsamic vinegar

Ingredients:

- 500g semolina
- 300ml of warm water
- 80ml of balsamic vinegar
- 7g dry yeast or fresh
- 1 tablespoon vegetable oil
- 2 teaspoons of salt
- 1.5 teaspoons ground parsley
- 1.5 teaspoon ground cumin
- 2 tablespoons whole cumin seed

Preparation:

Grind semolina in a coffee grinder. Balsamic vinegar boils until reduced in volume by half. Cool to room temperature. In a container with warm water, stir the yeast until it dissolves completely.

Ground the mango through a sieve into a bowl. Then add salt, ground coriander and ground cumin. Then pour in the yeast water, boiled vinegar and vegetable oil. Stir the dough by hand for about 20 minutes until elasticity. Dough covers with a towel and leave to go for 1.5-2 hours.

Approached the dough and wrap it in a greased form. Cover the dough in a towel and leave for an hour for proofing. After proofing, sprinkle the surface of the product with warm water and sprinkle with seeds of cumin.

Bake in preheated to t = 160C oven for 35 minutes, then another 15 minutes at t = 180C. Finished bread to get from the oven, remove from the form and wrapped in a towel to leave for the night. On the second day of bread is more delicious.

Mustard Grissini

Ingredients:

- 120 ml of water
- 250 g of wheat flour
- 1/2 pack of dry yeast
- 1 teaspoon of salt
- 1 tablespoon sugar
- 5 tablespoons of olive oil
- 2 tablespoons of ready-made mustard
- 1 onion
- Sesame

Preparation:

Fry finely chopped onion with olive oil. Knead the dough from flour, yeast, warm water, salt, sugar, mustard and fried onions. A good knead and you can immediately form sticks. From the dough to tear off small pieces and in the hands to roll thin sticks about 25-30 cm long and 1-1.5 cm thick. Put a handful of sesame on the food foil or other surface and roll every stick in it.

Put the sticks on a baking sheet covered with baking paper, bake in a preheated oven 190 degrees for about 15-20 minutes until golden brown.

Baursak is round

Ingredients:
- Wheat flour - 400 g
- Milk - 2 cups
- Margarine - 2 tablespoons
- Yeast - 5-6 g
- Sugar - 2 tablespoons
- Salt - 1 teaspoon
- Vegetable oil - 800 ml

Preparation:

In warm milk, dilute the yeast with sugar and salt. Set aside for 15 minutes. Add the softened margarine, the sifted flour and knead the dough, after adding the vegetable oil and knead well.

Close the lid or food film tightly with a cup of dough. Cover with a towel and put in a warm place for 40-45 minutes. The dough should come up twice. From the dough, separate a small piece and roll the sausage out of it. Rib palm sprinkle with flour and, making translational movements, separate small pieces the size of a walnut.

In a cauldron it is good to warm up oil. Put on medium fire and spread out Baursak for 12-15 pieces at a time. During the roasting, stir the Baursak constantly. Finished Baursak place on a paper towel to remove excess oil.

Piglet with cocoa and strawberry jam

Ingredients:

- Puff pastry 0,5 leaves
- 2 tablespoons cocoa
- Strawberry jam

Preparation:

The dough is divided into 6 identical parts. To 2 add a spoon of cocoa and mix. We make 6 thin sausages. We connect at the base of 3 sausages and plait pigtail, using 2 of a puff pastry without cocoa, and one with cocoa.

Put the pigtail in the form, lubricate the protein and put in the oven for 20 minutes. Serve with strawberry or any other jam.

Borodino bread in the bread maker

Ingredients:

- Malt rye 30 g
- Boiling water 100 ml
- Rye peeled flour 200 g
- Whole meal flour 200 g
- Yeast 1.2 teaspoon
- Salt 1 teaspoon
- Sugar 1 tablespoon
- Water 220 g
- Vinegar wine or dry wine 20 g
- Coriander 1 teaspoon
- Vegetable oil 1 tablespoon
- Raisins 30 g

Preparation:

Malt pours boiling water, stir and cool. Coriander is ground in a mortar. Mix two varieties of flour, raisins and coriander. In the bakery to lay food according to the instructions, first go dry ingredients, then, liquid. First put the yeast, then flour. On top of the flour add salt and sugar, pour out the malt and water, and add the vinegar and butter.

Wheat-rye yeast bread on brine

Ingredients:

- Brine from tomatoes or cucumbers 300 g
- Rye grain crushed 100 g
- Rye peeled flour 120 g
- Wheat flour 350 g
- Yeast powder 1,5 teaspoons
- Water 30 ml
- Salt 10 g
- Sugar 15 g
- Vegetable oil 1-2 teaspoons
- Cumin or sesame 1-2 teaspoons

Preparation:

Yeast with one teaspoon of sugar diluted in 30 ml of water. Wait for the yeast to foam. Rye grains grind roughly to pieces came across. Mix with rye flour. Brine slightly warmed, add salt and sugar. Add rye mixture, mix thoroughly and allow swelling for 20 minutes.

Pour the yeast mixture, gradually pour the wheat flour, and knead the soft, slightly sticky dough. Cover the dough and leave in a warm place for lifting. When the dough greatly increases in volume, divide it in half, spread out into shapes, greasing hands with vegetable oil. Sprinkle with caraway seeds or sesame seeds. Cover the forms with a packet and put in heat to raise the dough. It is necessary to wait for the moment when the dough rises as much as possible.

Bake at 190 degrees for about 40 minutes. Prepared bread with parchment from the forms, cover with a towel and a packet. Completely cool down.

A fragrant loaf

Ingredients:
- 450 g wheat flour
- 250 ml of water
- 1 teaspoon yeast dry
- 2 teaspoons of salt
- 2 tablespoons olive oil
- 50-80 g any hard cheese
- 3-5 g of dried dill
- 1 piece yolk
- Vegetable oil for lubricating a bowl and dough

Preparation:

1) Put the yeast in a glass of warm water and cover it with a food film, set aside until a frothy cap appears.

2) Sift the flour into a bowl, mix with water and water with yeast.

3) Add butter and knead soft, elastic dough.

4) Let's knead the dough for 10-15 minutes. It should become elastic and not stick to your hands. Lubricate the container for proofing with oil and lay out the dough, the surface of the dough will be oiled lightly. We will tighten a bowl with a test food film and we will put in a dark, warm place to approach. For an hour and a half.

5) When the dough rises at least twice - you can begin to form a loaf. The dough is kneaded and rolled into a rectangular bed.

6) Sprinkle with grated cheese and dried dill.

7) Fold the wide edges of the rectangle to the center.

8) Then again, and splinter the edges in the middle.

9) Lay out our loaf on a baking sheet covered with baking paper.

10) We make longitudinal incisions on the test and lubricate the yolk mixed with water. Let's give the loaf for 30 minutes to the proof.

11) Preheat the oven to 180-190 degrees. At the bottom of the pot must be filled with boiling water. Spray the oven on the walls and put our loaf on the middle level. We will bake for 20-30 minutes.

Bread plates

Ingredients:

- Flour - 500 g
- Salt - 1 teaspoon
- Sugar - 1.5 teaspoons
- Yeast - 2 teaspoons
- Milk - 160 ml
- Water - 160 ml
- Vegetable oil - 5 tablespoons
- Oil of the plant - 3 tablespoons
- Eggs - 1 piece
- Dill and parsley - 1 teaspoon
- Sugar - 2 tablespoons
- Cinnamon - ½ teaspoon

Preparation:

Sift flour into a bowl. Add salt, sugar and yeast. To stir thoroughly. Milk mixed with water and heated. To our flour add water with milk and butter. Carefully knead the dough to make a lump. Put in a warm place for 1 hour.

Approach the dough to knead and lightly knead. Roll it on a flour-poured table into a square measuring 30x25 cm, put it on a baking sheet and let it go again for 30-40 minutes. The egg is mixed with butter. Lubricate ½ part of this mixture with our dough.

Cut the dough into slices. Once again, grease the tiles with an egg-and-oil mixture. ½ a portion of the slices sprinkle with dill and parsley, and the other with sugar and cinnamon. Bake in a preheated 200 degrees oven for 35-40 minutes.

Rye bread with oat flakes

Ingredients:

- Rye flour - 200 g
- Wheat Flour - 185 g
- Oatmeal - 3 tablespoons
- Yeast - 1 and 3/4 teaspoon
- Salt - 1.5 teaspoons
- Sugar - 1 and 3/4 tablespoons
- Vegetable oil - 2 tablespoons
- Water - 290 ml
- Malt - 2 tablespoons

Preparation:

Pour malt with hot water 70-80 ml, stir and cool to room temperature. The total water should be 290 ml. In the bread maker, put the ingredients according to the instructions.

Blade for kneading put on rye bread. Baking mode - rye bread (3.5 hours).

German festive bread

Ingredients:

- 1 teaspoon with a slide dry for yeast
- 1 cup of milk
- 4 tablespoons butter
- 2 tablespoons of sugar
- 2 eggs
- 2 teaspoons of salt
- 4¼ cups of flour

Preparation:

Dissolve the yeast in 0.5 cups of milk, leave for 10 minutes. The rest of the milk should be heated with sugar and butter on a small fire. Sift the flour into a bowl, add salt, make a groove in the middle and pour in milk and butter and a yeast mixture + lightly beaten eggs.

Knead the dough. Knead for 10 minutes. It turns out soft slightly sticky dough. Leave the dough in a warm place for 1.5 hours. The batter should be left to rest for 10 minutes. Divide into 19 possibly equal balls. Put in a circle shape: 12 balls + 6 balls + 1 ball in the center.

Cover with cellophane and leave for 45 minutes. Lubricate the top with a mixture of yolk and 1 tablespoon of water. Sprinkle with sesame seeds, poppy seeds, sea salt. Bake in preheated oven for about 40 minutes, until golden brown.

Drunken buns, on beer

Ingredients:
- 400 g of flour
- 1 package of baking powder
- 1 teaspoon of salt
- 1 teaspoon sugar
- 50 g of butter
- 300 ml of beer

Preparation:

Sifted flour, baking powder, salt and sugar mixed in one cup. Add oil and grind a little. Now gradually pour in the beer and knead the dough. Beer is added until the dough leaves the cup. Dough lies on the flour-strewn table and knead a little.

Heat the oven with the upper and lower heating to 210 degrees. In the oven in the bottom put a cup of boiling water, to increase the humidity in the oven. The dough is divided into 8 equal parts, we form round buns, we spread them on a baking sheet covered with baking paper.

Buns cut along the length of about 0.5 cm deep and lubricate them with water. We bake buns at 210 degrees for about 25 minutes.

Wheat corn baguette

Ingredients:

- White flour 400 g
- Corn flour 100 g
- Yeast, fresh 25 g
- Mineral water with gas 300 ml
- Olive oil 2 cups
- Salt 2 teaspoons
- Honey liquid 2 teaspoons
- Oregano Dried 1 teaspoon
- Chili
- Corn flour 1-2 tablespoons
- Olive oil 1-2 tablespoons

Preparation:

In the mineral water, dissolve the honey and dissolve the yeast. In a container, combine all the flour, salt, oregano and chili. Add the mineral water with yeast and olive oil, knead the dough and put in heat for an hour.

Ready to knead the dough again and split it in half. One part is rolled into a layer, rolled into a roll and put on a parchment, sprinkled with flour, with a seam down.

So do with the second part. Cover the baguettes with a towel and -in heat for an hour. Then cut them with scissors, grease with olive oil and sprinkle with corn flour. To send in an oven heated up to 220 degrees for 20-25 minutes. Let's cool it on the grate.

Just bread

Ingredients:
- 3 cups flour
- 1.5 teaspoons of salt
- 1.5 cups of water
- ¼ teaspoon dried yeast

Preparation:

Sift flour and pour into a bowl. Put the salt, dry yeast. Gradually pour water and stir the flour until all the water has absorbed. Do not interfere.

Cover the food film with dishes and leave until the morning. Form bread, cover and leave to go for 2 hours. Heat the oven to 230 degrees. Bake preferably in a container with a lid, making a top cover from the foil.

We put bread, cover with a lid and bake under the lid for 25 minutes. We remove the lid; sprinkle the top with preferably rye flour or wheat flour and another 15-20 minutes. Very tasty bread with large holes.

Focaccia with cheese from brewed dough

Ingredients:

- 250 g of flour
- 300 ml of water
- 125 g of butter
- 4 eggs
- 250 g of cheese
- A pinch of salt
- Sun dried cherry tomatoes

Preparation:

Boil water with oil, add flour and whisk the dough until it leaves the walls. Dough a little cold and one by one enter the eggs, all the time continuously whipped. Add the cheese, cut into small cubes, a little for decoration.

The form is lubricated with oil, we spread the dough, level it and sprinkle the remaining cubes of cheese, decorate with tomatoes. Bake at 200 degrees for 20 minutes, then reduce the heat to 180 degrees and bake another 15 minutes.

"Monkey bread"

Ingredients:

- 1.5 cups of water
- 4 tablespoons butter
- 4 cups of flour
- 3 tablespoons milk powder
- 4 tablespoons sugar
- 1 teaspoon of salt
- 2 teaspoons fast dry yeast
- Bunches of parsley and dill
- 1 slice
- 1/4 teaspoon of salt
- 5 tablespoons of butter
- 100 g of cheese

Preparation:

Prepare the yeast dough: mix sugar, salt, milk powder and yeast. Add the sifted flour, stir. Then water, mix again, add oil and knead the dough. If it's liquid, add a little more flour. Form a ball and beat it against the table for a few minutes. We send the dough to go up.

Finished father-in-law is divided into balls the size of a large walnut. Prepare the mixture: finely chop the greens of parsley and dill, let the garlic through the press, and melt the butter. All mixed, add salt. Each "nut" is dipped in this mixture. Lay the first layer of the balls in the shape. Sprinkle a layer of balls with grated cheese, and then put the balls again.

Cover the form. The product should increase in volume in 2 times. This takes approximately 30-45 minutes. Put the form in a preheated oven and bake at 190 degrees 40 minutes until golden brown. After baking bread, sorted into portions.

Pseudo - Borodinsky loaf

Ingredients:

- 1/4 cup of milk
- 1 tablespoon of black leaf tea
- 1 glass of mineral water with gas
- 2 tablespoons coriander seeds
- 1.5 teaspoons dried yeast
- 1 teaspoon of shallow salt
- 1.5 tablespoons brown sugar
- 1.5 teaspoons balsamic vinegar
- 1 teaspoon of liquid honey
- 1 tablespoon of sunflower oil
- ¾ cup of rye flour
- 1 1/3 of wheat flour

Preparation:

Brew tea in hot milk, mix with mineral water, when it cools down - strain. Calcify the coriander in a dry frying pan, crush it into powder. Sift the flour. Mix all the ingredients including tea and coriander

Well knead the dough Place the dough in a bowl for proofing, cover, put it in a warm place and let it come up 2 times. Form a loaf, give it a go. Sprinkle the top lightly with rye flour. Oven for 200 degrees. Bake for 30-40 minutes.

Long bread

Ingredients:

Whole-wheat flour 100 g

White flour 150 g

Salt 1 teaspoon

Yeast, fresh 12 g

Soft butter 20 g

Milk powder 10 g

Honey 1 teaspoon

Water cold 125 ml

Preparation:

Of all the ingredients knead the dough, close the film and put in the fridge for two hours. Then divide it into 8-10 parts. Parchment we will add an accordion so that there are so many grooves, how many sausages you wind from the dough, I have 8 pieces.

Lay the sausages in the grooves, smearing the parchment with a little oil. We put in heat for an hour. Preheat the oven to 250 degrees, bake for 7-10 minutes, depending on the thickness of the loaves.

Lacy oriental bread

Ingredients:

Flour about 3 cups

Water warm 1 glass

Yeast, fresh 25 g

Sugar 1 teaspoon

1/3 teaspoon salt

Olive oil 2 tablespoons

Preparation:

In warm water with sugar, dissolve the yeast, add flour, salt and 1 tablespoon of olive oil, knead docile, like plasticine, dough.

We lubricate the container with the remaining oil, put the dough there and put it in the heat for an hour and a half. Then we need it a little, divide it into 6 parts.

We roll each into a cake with a diameter of about 20 cm. using a sharp knife, we make deep incisions. Preheat the oven to 275 degrees; bake 2-3 minutes on each side.

Paljanica

Ingredients:

900g of wheat flour

200ml of milk

300ml of water

2 tablespoons of sugar

2 packets of dry yeast

100g butter

1 tablespoon of salt

Vegetable oil for mold lubrication

Preparation:

Put the spit. Mix 300ml of warm water, yeast, sugar and 100g of flour, put in a warm place and leave to wander about two hours. At the end of time, knead the dough, adding all the remaining products. And put it up in the form in which you will bake bread in a warm place for another couple of hours, during this time, double-press the dough. When you knead the dough the second time, separate ¼ of the dough. Leave the most part up in the form, and the smaller part in the other vessel. When the dough in the pan increases, make a small groove in the center and place the separated part there.

Put the form in a hot oven and bake for 35-40 minutes. The top crust should brighten well, and in the place where the flat cake was laid, a rupture is formed. Take the bread out of the mold; allow it to cool on the grate.

Cakes with poppy seeds

Ingredients:

- 470-500 g of flour
- 220 ml of mineral water with gas
- 6 g dry yeast
- 1 small egg
- 75 g of butter
- 3 teaspoons salt
- 1 tablespoon sugar
- 1 egg yolk stirs with a spoon of water
- Poppy

Preparation:

Grind the yeast with sugar and dissolve half the water and let stand for 10 minutes. Beat the eggs lightly together with the second part of the water. Mix yeast with water and sift half the flour. Mix thoroughly and leave the sponge for 30-40 minutes in a warm place until the bubbles appear.

Sift the rest of the flour into a spoon, and knead elastic dough, adding salt and oil at the end. Put into a greased bowl and leave to stand for 30 minutes. Divide the dough into 4-5 parts and roll it into loaves about 2 cm thick. Cover with a foil and leave to stand for another 30 minutes.

Lubricate with a yolk, whipped with water, pierce with a fork in several places and sprinkle with poppy seeds. Bake at 200 degrees for 15 minutes.

Home Bread "Fitness"

Ingredients:

- 600 g of flour
- 625 ml of water
- 30 g fresh or 20 g dry yeast
- 2 tablespoons of sugar
- 2 tablespoons of salt
- 1 glass of bran
- 3 handfuls of multi-cereal flakes
- 1 large carrot
- 1 teaspoon of cumin
- 0,5 glasses of vegetable oil

Preparation:

Mix flour with bran and cereal. Yeast dilute with a little warm water. Further in the water to dissolve salt and sugar. Slowly pour the water into the flour, add the vegetable oil and mix the dough, pouring flour into the water from the edges. Grate the carrots and add them to the dough. Add the cumin. Dough well until the dough begins to fall behind. If the flour is small, add a little. Next, the dough should be covered with a towel and put in a warm, non-blowing place for 40-60 minutes. After the dough has increased in volume, knead it and put it on a baking sheet, sprinkled with flour. Again, cover with a napkin and let it come. The oven is heated up to 200 degrees. We put the baking sheet with bread, reduce the power of the oven to 170 degrees and bake for 1 hour. After the bread is ready, we remove it from the oven, moisten the crust with water and cover with a towel.

Bread Darnytskyi

Ingredients:

- Flour rye - 325g
- Wheat Flour - 225g
- Malt - 4 tablespoons
- Honey or sugar - 2 tablespoons
- Salt - 1.5 teaspoons
- Vegetable oil - 2 tablespoons
- Cumin - 1 tablespoon
- Yeast - 2 tablespoons
- Water boiling water - 80ml
- Water - 330ml

Preparation:

Pour the malt with boiling water and let it cool down. Put all the dry ingredients in the bucket, spread the brewed malt and pour in the water and oil. When you test, the bread maker needs your help. Take a plastic narrow shoulder blade or something suitable for this.

Turn on the "No Gluten" mode, the bread maker will immediately begin to interfere, after a couple of minutes, help from the corners of the bucket to clean the flour to a common lump, help stir for 2-3 minutes. Once you start this program, set the alarm for an hour, after this time, you need to turn off the "Gluten-free" mode.

Dough for an hour is already good enough and tries not to slam the lid, looking inside, that it would not settle. Now turn on the "Baking" mode, set the time to 1 hour and 30 minutes and wait for the result.

Bread yoghurt-milk with dried fruits

Ingredients:

- 200 ml of yogurt
- 150 ml of milk
- 550 g of wheat flour
- 50 g butter
- 1.5 teaspoons of salt
- 2 tablespoons of sugar
- 1 2 \ 3 teaspoons of yeast
- Raisins, cranberries and strawberries - 1 cup measuring

Preparation:

Everything is laid in the bread maker according to the instructions in your bread maker. At first everything is liquid.

Salt, sugar and yeast measured with a measuring spoon from the bread maker. Dried fruits all washed and dried with a paper towel. Add after the first batch, when there will be an audible signal.

Mini-tortillas with eggplant, paprika and olives

Ingredients:

- 1 teaspoon of yeast
- 1.5 teaspoons of salt
- 1.5 tablespoons of sugar
- 150 g of flour
- 200 g of mango
- 1 tablespoon vegetable oil
- 280 ml of water
- 50 grams of grated cheese Gouda
- 100 grams of mini eggplant
- 1 teaspoon of olive oil
- 3-4 tablespoons of olives without pits
- 3 cloves of garlic
- Paprika
- Provencal herbs with garlic and pepper
- Salt, sugar to taste

Preparation:

All the dry ingredients for the dough put in a bowl, add the vegetable oil and water, mix.

Cover the bowl with a film, put in a warm place for 45 minutes. Lubricate the dough with olive oil, form 6 identical koloboks. Cover the pan with baking paper. Form oval tortillas, lay on a baking tray, cover with a film and leave for 45 minutes in a warm place. Pepper to cut finely, garlic with thin plates, olives with rings. Eggplants cut, sprinkle with salt and sugar, leave for 30 minutes, then rinse with cold water, dry, lightly fry in olive oil. In the middle of the tortillas make a groove, so that around the circle was a small side, sprinkle with grated cheese, lay eggplant, paprika, garlic, olives, and sprinkle with Provencal herbs. Bake in preheated oven at 200 degrees until cooked.

Basic bread recipe

Ingredients:

- 3 cups flour
- 310 ml of warm water
- 1 sachet of yeast
- 1 tablespoon sugar
- 1 tablespoon of sea salt

Preparation:

Pour flour on the hill and in the middle make a groove. In the groove carefully pour the water, pour in the yeast, salt and sugar. Gently stir the yeast, salt and sugar with a fork. Carefully we will collect the flour with our hands from the edges and gently add to the middle, stirring. When the dough absorbs all the water, add the rest of the water and mix.

We beat out the table, lie-twist, and finally achieve that the dough does not stick to your hands. Now cover with a film and put it in a warm place for 1.5 - 2 hours. Then thirty seconds we will crumple and twist the dough, knocking out air from it.

Put it in the mold and put it in a warm place without drafts until it is doubled. The oven is heated to 200 degrees. Bake, pre-lubricating the top with a yolk in half with water, until the top is well bruised - 35 minutes. Remove from the mold and put on a grate for 30 minutes.

Challah

Ingredients:

- Yeast high-speed 1.5 teaspoons
- Flour, wheat 400 g
- Flour, rice 100 g
- Salt 1.5 teaspoons
- Honey 2 tablespoons
- Butter 40 g
- Milk 350 ml
- Poppy
- Sesame

Preparation:

So lay the ingredients in the order in which they are described in the bread oven. Dough mode. Put the finished dough.

Divide the dough into 2 parts, then each part for another three. Weave two pigtails, hide the tips of the dough down, grease with milk and sprinkle with poppy seeds and sesame seeds. Allow to stand for another 20 minutes 20. Bake in a preheated oven to 220 degrees for 20-23 minutes. Put the chalices out of the form, cool on the grill, covered with a towel.

Cat "Matroskin"

Ingredients:

- 500g flour
- 1 egg
- Vegetable oil
- Water
- Salt and sugar to taste
- Sugar liqueur
- Strong coffee
- Dye

Preparation:

We need a steep dough, cut out the cat's figurine and bake first at 50 degrees with the door ajar, then another half an hour with the oven closed at 100 degrees.

We color the cat with sugar liqueur, strong coffee and dyes.

Dough, pies, pizza ...

Ingredients:

- 500 g of yogurt
- 200 g sour cream
- 2 packs of baking powder
- 2 eggs
- A pinch of salt
- Flour

Preparation:

Of the listed ingredients knead medium-mass dough, with the addition of flour to focus on the eye, the dough should be soft, allow it to stand for 2-3 hours, then you can start the needlework, this dough the longer lies, the better. Suitable for pies and pizza.

Italian bread

Ingredients:

- Wheat Flour 480 g
- Yeast fast - 0.5 tablespoons
- Salt 0,5 tablespoons
- Olive oil 1 tablespoon
- Water 400 g
- Dry basil 0.5 teaspoons
- Dry paprika 0.5 teaspoons

Preparation:

Mix flour with yeast and place them in a bucket with a baking oven, pour water. Stir to make all flour wet and leave for 20 minutes. Knead for 30 minutes, pour salt, basil, paprika in the middle of the batch, then add the vegetable oil by drop at the end of the batch. Put in a greased bowl; oil the top of the dough.

Cover and leave the dough to wander until it grows in volume by half. Put the dough in a mold, or in a cup, and leave to proof.

Turn on the oven for 250 degrees. Put in it a thick cast-iron frying pan and heat for 30 minutes. Approached the dough carefully put on the heated frying pan.

Bake for the first 10 minutes with the steam! Then reduce the temperature in the oven to 230 degrees and oven for 40 minutes.

Italian ciabatta bread

Ingredients:

- 1.5 cups of water
- 1.5 tablespoons sugar
- 50 g of raw yeast
- 3 tablespoons flour
- 4 cups of flour
- 0.5 cup olive oil
- A pinch of salt
- Fried onions

Preparation:

Knead the spoon from warm water, sugar, yeast and flour. Allow to simmer for 15 minutes. Then add the rest of the flour, butter and salt. Mix with your favorite additives.

We form bread. Knife we make notches. We bake for 20-30 minutes. The thinner the bread the less the baking time.

Khrushchev's dough sticks

Ingredients:

- 6 g dry yeast
- 1 tablespoon sugar
- 200 ml of milk
- 150 g of margarine
- 1 egg
- 1 teaspoon of salt
- 0.5 kg of flour
- Egg for lubrication

Preparation:

Milk warm to body temperature. Mix yeast with sugar, add a little milk and leave for 7-8 minutes. Margarine cut into pieces, put in a saucepan, melts over low heat and lightly cools.

Sift flour, add yeast, margarine, egg, salt to it and mix soft dough with milk. Flour - how much will it take. Put the dough in a spacious bowl - under the film of it, and in the fridge. The oven does not come back for more than an hour.

Paper for baking grease with vegetable oil, form a product on it, grease it with an egg. Bake at a temperature of 200-210 degrees to a rosy color.

Mustard bread

Ingredients:

- Dry yeast 1 teaspoon
- Flour, wheat 450 g
- Salt 1 teaspoon
- Sugar 2 tablespoons
- Mustard in powder 1 teaspoon
- Butter 20 g
- Mustard oil 2 tablespoons
- Milk 300 ml

Preparation:

Download the products to the bread maker in accordance with the instructions. The mode is "basic", the size is "M", and the crust is "medium".

Then take the dough out of the bucket, divide into 6 equal koloboks, roll them into round buns and put them in a greased form. Make a cut on each bun with a pair of scissors crosswise. Let stand a little, at room temperature, with a towel.

Bake at 200 degrees for about 40 minutes. Then pull the bread out of the mold, cover with a towel and allow cooling.

Sweet Arabic bread

Ingredients:

- 2/3 tablespoons yeast
- 450 g of flour
- 0.5 teaspoon of salt
- 40 g butter 80 ml
- Condensed milk 2 tablespoons of sugar
- 1/3 cup raisins
- 1 egg
- 200 ml of water

Preparation:

We put the products in the form of a bread maker and put it on the "Dough" mode. We take out the dough, form the balls and roll them in a mixture of sugar and cinnamon. We remove the spatula from the shape of the bread oven and tightly lay the balls. We give 40 minutes to go, put on the "Bake" mode.

Focaccia with black olives

Ingredients:

- 250 g of flour
- 1 teaspoon dried yeast
- 1 teaspoon sugar
- ½ teaspoon of salt
- 10-15 olives
- 2 tablespoons of olive oil
- 150 g of mineral water
- 300 g of tomato
- 100 grams of Suluguni cheese

Preparation:

Yeast diluted in a small amount of warm mineral water, add sugar and let stand for 10 minutes. Pour in the remaining water, add flour in portions and knead elastic dough. At the end, add salt and olive oil. Form a ball from the dough and put it in a greased dish. Cover, put in heat for 1 hour.

Form small cakes in the middle to put a circle of chopped tomato and a few circles of olives. Cover with plastic cheese. Cover with a film and let stand for another 30 minutes. Lubricate the focaccia with olive oil. Bake in preheated oven at 240 degrees 18 minutes.

Bread, Mediterranean

Ingredients:

- 450 ml of warm water
- 700 g of flour
- 1 pack of dry yeast
- 2 tablespoons olive oil
- 2 tablespoons of sugar
- 1 teaspoon of salt
- 2 teaspoons of a mixture of dried herbs
- Protein of one egg
- ½ teaspoon herbal mixture
- a pinch of large sea salt

Preparation:

The dough is unpaired. In order to prepare it you must mix all the ingredients. This can be done with the help of hands, a mixer, a kitchen machine or a bread maker in dough mode. If you cook the dough not in the bread maker, then put the dough in a warm place and let it come up, crushing a couple of times, if in the bread maker, then it will do it for you.

Ready to put the dough on a plentifully floured surface, divided into two parts, to form small loaves of bread and leave for 15 minutes to rest.

Bake in a hot oven, first at a temperature of 150 degrees 30 minutes, then increase the temperature to 180 degrees and finish browning for about 10-15 minutes, 5 minutes before readiness to take out bread, grease whipped with the addition of dry herbs protein, sprinkle with large sea salt and oven for 5 more minutes. Take the bread out of the oven and cool it on the grate. With this method of cooling from the crust, excess moisture is released and it remains crispy.

Christmas bread

Ingredients:

- 5 1/2 glasses of flour
- 0.5 cups of sugar
- 1 teaspoon of salt
- 1/4 teaspoon of nutmeg
- 1/4 teaspoon cinnamon
- 1 cup warm milk
- 150 g of butter, dissolve on fire
- 25 g yeast
- 3 eggs
- Raisins
- Dried cranberries
- 1 glass of brandy
- Grated peel 1 orange
- Powdered sugar for sprinkling

Preparation:

Yeast diluted in a few tablespoons of warm water. Wait for me to stand up. Mix with half the amount of flour, eggs, milk, spices, butter, sugar, salt. Leave to stand for two hours. Raisin and cranberries pour brandy and leave.

After two hours add the remaining flour, soaked dried fruit. Make bread in the form of pigtail, grease the egg and bake for about half an hour or forty minutes. When serving sprinkle with powdered sugar.

Tartin with garlic butter

Ingredients:

- 50 grams of garlic
- 300 g of butter
- 0.5 teaspoon ground white pepper
- 0.5 teaspoon ground ginger
- 3 tablespoons cream cheese
- 3 sprigs of dill
- Salt
- 4 cups of flour
- 10 g fresh yeast
- 1 cup of garlic butter
- 1 teaspoon of salt
- 1 glass of warm water

Preparation:

Slightly softened butter with crushed garlic, add salt to taste and season. Heat the oven to 200 degrees and turn it off. Spread the beaten oil 30 minutes. Cool it down. Add cream cheese, finely chopped dill and beat until lush.

A glass of millet flour and yeast thoroughly rub it with your hands. Pour warm water and whip. Put for 20 minutes in a warm place. Add the oil to the pan, add the oil, and mix thoroughly. Pour in the salt and, gradually pouring the remaining flour, knead the smooth dough. Put in a warm place on the approach for 40 minutes. From the dough, mold the baguettes, make a few incisions with a knife and leave under a damp towel for another 45 minutes for lifting. Lubricate with a brush with ice water and bake in a preheated oven for 200 minutes 25 minutes.

Copyright: Published in the United States by Teresa Moore / © Teresa Moore All Rights Reserved. No part of this publication or the information in it may be quoted from or reproduced in any form by means such as printing, scanning, photocopying or otherwise without prior written permission of the copyright holder. Disclaimer and Terms of Use: Effort has been made to ensure that the information in this book is accurate and complete, however, the author and the publisher do not warrant the accuracy of the information, text and graphics contained within the book due to the rapidly changing nature of science, research, known and unknown facts and internet. The Author and the publisher do not hold any responsibility for errors, omissions or contrary interpretation of the subject matter herein. This book is presented solely for motivational and informational purposes only.

Italian Bread

1. Easy Italian Bread

Ingredients

1 (1/4-ounce) envelope active dry yeast

1 teaspoon sugar

1 cup warm water (100° to 110°)

2 to 3 cups bread flour

2 tablespoons olive oil

1 teaspoon salt

Instructions

Combine yeast, sugar, and 1 cup warm water in bowl of a heavy-duty electric stand mixer; let stand 5 minutes. Add 2 cups flour, oil, and salt to bowl, and beat at low speed, using dough hook attachment, 1 minute. Gradually add additional flour until dough begins to leave the sides of the bowl and pull together. (Note: The dough will take on a "shaggy" appearance as the flour is being added. When enough flour has been added, the dough will look soft and smooth, not wet and sticky or overly dry with a rough surface.)

Increase speed to medium, and beat 5 minutes. Cover bowl of dough with plastic wrap, and let stand in a warm place (85°), free from drafts, 30 minutes or until doubled in bulk. Punch dough down, and let stand 10 minutes.

Turn dough out onto a lightly floured surface; shape dough into a 12-inch loaf, and place on a lightly greased baking sheet. Cut 3 (1/4-inch deep) slits across top of dough with a sharp paring knife. (The slits release interior steam and prevent the loaf from blowing apart at the side.)

Bake at 400° for 16 minutes or until golden brown. Cool on a wire rack.

Herbed Focaccia: Proceed with recipe as directed, shaping dough into a ball instead of a loaf. Roll dough into an 11- x 14-inch rectangle on a lightly greased baking sheet. Press handle of a wooden spoon into dough to make indentations at 1-inch intervals. Drizzle dough evenly with 1 tablespoon olive oil; sprinkle evenly with 1 teaspoon dried Italian seasoning. Bake at 475° for 12 to 15 minutes or until golden brown.

Pizza Crust: Proceed with recipe as directed, shaping dough into a ball instead of a loaf. Roll dough into an 11- x 14-inch rectangle on a lightly greased baking sheet. Drizzle with olive oil, or spread with pesto or pizza sauce, and sprinkle with desired toppings. Bake at 475° for 20 to 25 minutes.

2. Mom's Italian Bread Recipe

Ingredients

1 package (1/4 ounce) active dry yeast

2 cups warm water (110° to 115°)

1 teaspoon sugar

2 teaspoons salt

5-1/2 cups all-purpose flour

Instructions

In a large bowl, dissolve yeast in warm water. Add the sugar, salt and 3 cups flour. Beat on medium speed for 3 minutes. Stir in remaining flour to form a soft dough.

Turn onto a floured surface; knead until smooth and elastic, about 6-8 minutes. Place in a greased bowl, turning once to grease the top. Cover and let rise in a warm place until doubled, about 1 hour.

Punch dough down. Turn onto a floured surface; divide in half. Shape each portion into a loaf. Place each loaf seam side down on a greased baking sheet. Cover and let rise until doubled, about 30 minutes.

Meanwhile, preheat oven to 400°. With a sharp knife, make four shallow slashes across top of each loaf. Bake 20-25 minutes or until golden brown. Remove from pans to wire racks to cool.

Yield: 2 loaves (12 slices each).

3. Rustic Italian Bread

Ingredients

3 to 3 1/2 cups Pillsbury BEST™ Bread Flour

2 teaspoons sugar

1/2 teaspoon salt

1 (1/4 oz.) packet active dry yeast

1 cup warm water (120 to 130°F)

2 tablespoons Crisco® Pure Olive Oil

Crisco® Original No-Stick Cooking Spray

1 tablespoon cornmeal

1 egg white, beaten

Instructions

STIR flour, sugar, salt and yeast in large bowl. Mix well. Add warm water and oil. Mix well. Turn dough out onto lightly floured surface. Knead until smooth and elastic, about 10 minutes, adding additional flour as necessary. Coat large bowl with no-stick cooking spray. Place dough in bowl, turning to coat top. Cover loosely with plastic wrap. Let rise in warm place until doubled in size, about 30 to 40 minutes.

SPRINKLE baking sheet with cornmeal. Punch down dough. Shape dough into oval-shaped loaf, about 12 inches long. Place on prepared baking sheet. Cover loosely with greased plastic wrap. Let rise in warm place until doubled in size, about 30 to 45 minutes.

HEAT oven to 375°F. Make a 1-inch deep lengthwise slash in top of loaf using a serrated knife.

Brush loaf with egg white. Bake 30 to 35 minutes or until loaf sounds hollow when lightly tapped.

4. Sourdough Ciabatta Italian Bread

Ingredients

1 cup sourdough starter, room temperature

3/4 cup warm water (110 degrees F.)

2 tablespoons extra-virgin olive oil

1 1/2 teaspoons salt

1 tablespoon granulated sugar

1 1/2 cups bread flour or unbleached all-purpose flour

1/2 cup semolina flour

1/2 teaspoon diastatic malt (optional)

1 teaspoon instant yeast

Instructions

Place all ingredients in bread pan of your bread machine. Select dough setting and press start. When dough cycle has finished, dough will be very soft (between a batter and a runny dough). Remove dough from pan and place into a oiled large bowl. Cover with plastic wrap and let rise in at room temperature approximately 1 1/2 hours or until tripled in bulk (dough will be sticky and full of bubbles).

On a baking sheet, place a sheet of parchment paper. Sprinkle parchment paper with semolina flour. Turn the risen dough onto a flour dusted work surface. Pat dough (do not punch down) into a rectangle and dust with flour. Transfer to prepared baking sheet. Press fingertips into dough in several places to dimple surface. Cover dough with plastic wrap and let rise at room temperature for 1 1/2 to 2 hours or until doubled in bulk.

At least 45 minutes before baking, place baking stones on lowest oven rack in oven and set the temperature to 500 degrees F. Allow the oven to heat for 30 minutes.

Lower oven temperature to 400 degrees F. Transfer loaf (with parchment paper) to the hot baking stones. Bake 15 minutes or until pale golden. A good check is to use an instant digital thermometer to test your bread. The internal temperature should be between 200 and 210 degrees F.

Remove from oven and place the bread on a wire rack to cool. Let baked loaf cool for 30 minutes before cutting (this is because the bread is still cooking while it is cooling).

5. Italian Cheese Bread

Ingredients

2 (1/4 oz.) pkg. dry yeast

1 cup margarine

6 large eggs

4 1/2 cups all-purpose flour -- sifted

1 tsp. salt

2 tsp. sugar

1/4 lb. Swiss cheese

1/4 lb. sharp cheddar cheese

1/2 cup Parmesan cheese – grated

Instructions

Dissolve yeast in 1 cup of warm water.

In a large mixing bowl, beat margarine until fluffy. Beat eggs in another bowl until light. Add eggs to margarine, blending well. Stir in dissolved yeast water.

Sift flour, salt and sugar together. Gradually add to egg mixture, continue to beat until satiny.

Cut Swiss and Cheddar cheese into 1/4 inch cubes. Stir cubed cheese and Parmesan cheese into mixture.

Place dough in a 4 quart greased glass mixing bowl. Cover and let rise until doubled in volume.

With spoon, and stir gently. Cover bowl and let rise until doubled, again.

Grease a 10-inch tube pan. Gently stir dough down. Pour into pan. Let rise again until doubled.

Bake in a preheated 400 degrees oven for 35 - 40 minutes. Cool 10 minutes out of oven. Lift bread out by tube and cool 20 more minutes.

www.ingramcontent.com/pod-product-compliance
Lightning Source LLC
Chambersburg PA
CBHW071439070526
44578CB00001B/143